the armstrong error

by

C.F. DeLOACH

Logos International
Plainfield, New Jersey

THE ARMSTRONG ERROR

Unless otherwise identified, Scripture is quoted from the King James' Version of the Bible.

Printed in the United States of America
Logos International, Plainfield, New Jersey 07060

Library of Congress Catalog Card Number 73-129817
SBN 912106-13-1

"Herbert W. Armstrong's Radio Church of God, while appearing to be Christian, is in reality a perversion of Christianity. This is clearly revealed by the author who was a member of Armstrong's cult before his conversion. This book should be read by all Christians, and should be given to those who have become confused by Herbert W. Armstrong and the Radio Church of God."

James Bjornstad
Assistant Director
Christian Research Institute
Author of *20th Century Prophecy,
Jeane Dixon, Edgar Cayce*

"Charles F. DeLoach has produced a highly readable and thoughtful refutation of Armstrongism. He obviously possesses a deep concern for the souls of those who are being deluded by a cult which is a masterpiece of Satanic deceit, and his study will be of great value both to concerned Christians and to those who have been themselves deceived. Every evangelical Christian should read this book so that he may be prepared to help others who are less well informed."

Herbert Vander Lugt
Research Editor
Radio Bible Class
Grand Rapids, Michigan 49501

CONTENTS

ORIGIN AND GROWTH OF ARMSTRONG*ISM*

If their own figures are correct, *The World Tomorrow* broadcast is now being heard by "50 million people every week" over 329 radio stations worldwide and 38 television stations in the United States and Canada.

Their magazine, *The Plain Truth,* has a current circulation of 2,080,000, indicating a readership of over six million for each issue. Probably setting a new, all-time record for growth, the slick, color-illustrated magazine has doubled its pressrun in just the last two years alone. It is adding new readers to its mailing list at the average rate of 60,000 a month.

They have opened their own Ambassador College to provide their students with "a RIGHT and TRUE education." Today the college occupies three campuses, two in the United States and one in Great Britain. Their educational program extends far beyond these campuses, however. Their free Bible course "is disseminated into the homes, worldwide." This correspondence study, which they claim gives people actual "understanding" of the Bible "for the first time," now has an enrollment of "over 80,000 active students from around the world," who are "from all walks of life—factory workers, housewives, college students, lawyers, doctors, farmers—even ministers of religion."[1]

Moreover, by their latest published figures, the mail pouring into the Pasadena (Calif.) Post Office from their readers, listeners, and contributors had reached a "staggering total of 1,601,963 letters" in 1967, a figure that must be revised sharply upward in view of their rapidly expanding audience. A "letter answering" staff, composed of *ordained* ministers and graduate students, gives guidance to those who write in seeking answers to religious questions. [2]

All this has been the extraordinary achievement of one man—Herbert W. Armstrong. In little more than thirty-five years, the former advertising man turned minister has, through his own personal drive, indomitable will, and unflagging conviction, *built* one of the fastest growing religious sects in the world, one that today troubles the established church with its many unorthodox teachings.

By many concerned church leaders, Armstrong has been labeled a heretic.

And, from the very first, Armstrong has used his radio pulpit to frequently and vociferously declare that his church was the only *true* church and to denounce all others as counterfeits actually serving Satan, "DECEIVING the world—by substituting pagan beliefs while preaching ABOUT Christ!" [3]

His gospel is certainly different, and conflicts sharply with the traditional doctrines taught by the church today. And literally hundreds of thousands have believed. These have become fiercely dedicated to both the man and his cause. To him they tithe their money. Some indeed are so convinced of the validity of his calling that they have actually sold all they owned and given it over in order that the Armstrong gospel might reach many more people.

Needless to say, the sharp differences between Armstrong's message and the long-taught and accepted doctrines of the church have been on a collision course in many homes. Where Christian families were once at peace, all in agreement as to their religious beliefs and philosophy, there are now arguments, heartbreak, and division, for, by necessity, one side or the other in this question must be heretics, guilty of following false doctrines. As a result, a father is set against a son or daughter, a daughter against her mother, and, as it happens at times, a husband against the wife of his bosom. This is not only condoned by the Armstrong cult, it is both taught and encouraged (as we shall see later). To become a true disciple, they say, one must expect persecution from his own family, and also from former friends, this being in accordance with Jesus' prophecy in Matthew 10:36 (RSV), where it is declared: "...And a man's foes will be those of his own household." And when strife does begin, especially over the determination of one to attend Ambassador College against parental wishes, the one *confirmed* in the Armstrong faith feels that he has finally attained to *true* discipleship since he is now being "persecuted" by his very own family, *those of his own household,* in accordance with the Scriptures.

It is invariably true that the convert, as a result of the time he has spent studying under Armstrong's guidance, now knows more about the Bible than the other members of the churchgoing family, and so those who would attempt to expose the errors are immediately put at a very serious disadvantage. Usually, too, appeals to the clergy for help are just as useless, since many of the hometown ministers, although they have usually heard the name Armstrong and stand ready to condemn him, actually know very little about the man or what he teaches. Thus, in untold thousands of households, Armstrong has become a force to reckon with, and a source of grief in those in which the conversion is not unanimous. The problem is a growing one, and since large numbers are embracing these new doctrines each passing day, it becomes important to ask: who is this man who has managed quite successfully to present himself to millions as an authoritative teacher of the Word of God? And just what does he stand for?

Armstrong's beginning as a religious leader was humble enough. After a career in advertising and public relations work, mainly as an "idea man" for a trade publication called *The Merchant's Trade Journal,* he began what he calls his "transition from advertising into the ministry." [4]

It was not until 1934, however, on the very first Sunday

of the new year, that he was able to launch *The World Tomorrow* radio program which provided him with the springboard for his remarkable success. How did it come into being? On this, Armstrong relates that during the summer of 1933, while living in Oregon, he planned "a series of lectures" in and around Eugene, Oregon, and walked out over the countryside inviting neighbors to attend. "A little later," he adds, "an invitation came to lecture over radio." Afterward, the owner of the 100-watt station called him in and suggested a regular half-hour program, at a cost of only three dollars per half hour. "That," he writes, "was the start of *The World Tomorrow* program. It could not have started smaller." [5]

The following month, the first issue of *The Plain Truth* came off the press, or rather off "a borrowed mimeograph" machine.

Thus the first week of 1934 is an important date on the Armstrong calendar, in more respects than one. This was, Armstrong and his followers actually believe, one of the most important dates in all history, even though Armstrong says he was not even aware of its great significance at the time.

"On the first Sunday in 1934," he writes, "God's time had come. God opened a DOOR! Jesus Christ Himself had foretold this event! Millions have read his prophecy."

Yet "on that first Sunday in 1934, probably NO one—certainly not I myself—recognized what a momentous event actually was taking place.

"What really occurred that Sunday morning precisely at 10 o'clock, was a momentous event. It was the fulfilling of a definite cornerstone prophecy of Jesus.* More than that, it was the initial, start-off event of the fulfilling of some 90% of all the prophecies in the Bible! And approximately a third of the whole Bible is prophecy!" [6]

This occasion was also, in Armstrong's estimation, tremendously important for another reason. It was, he believes, the first time since 69 A.D. that the *true* gospel of

Christ had been heard. At that time, he maintains, the Romans were successful in stamping out the organized preaching of the gospel in any effective manner, and, as a result, professing Christians turned away from Christ's truth, and began embracing pagan fables. "From that time," he states, "the world has heard the name of Christ. The world has heard a Gospel of MEN ABOUT Christ. The world has called it 'The Gospel of Christ'—but it is very far from CHRIST'S Gospel—it is a paganized gospel of MEN ABOUT Christ. It is a counterfeit!" [7]

But where was the church all this time, the church of which Christ said that even the "gates of hell shall not prevail against it"?

In the wilderness, Armstrong answers.

"The prophecies bring this Church into concrete focus in the 12th chapter of Revelation," he declares. "There she is shown spiritually, in the glory and splendor of the Spirit of God, but visibly in the world as a persecuted, Commandment-keeping Church *driven into the wilderness,* for 1,260 years, through the middle ages!" [8]

This is the church, he claims, that made its appearance again on that first Sunday in January 1934. From 69 A.D., when the Romans "were successful in stamping out the organized preaching of the gospel," until the year 1934, when *The World Tomorrow* program started broadcasting, the world and all the generations from that time had not the *true* gospel of Christ preached to them.

Not many, by this account, will be able to inherit the kingdom promised by God, for the very reason that all went down to their graves lost, not having heard the true gospel. What has Armstrong to say about this?

It is taught by the Bible, he replies, that the *true* church would always be small in numbers. "Although Jesus said the gates of hell would never prevail against His Church," he adds, "yet it is everywhere prophesied through the New Testament as the 'Little Flock'—never as a great, large, popular universal church." [9] The 'Little Flock' that is *everywhere prophesied* in the Bible appears in the Scriptures but once. However, the Bible does teach that the church will be in the minority. The many, Jesus said, will take the broad way and enter the wide gate that leads to destruction, while the "way which leadeth unto life" is narrow and "strait is the gate. . .and few there be that find it." Still, these will be in much greater numbers than Armstrong comes close to anticipating. The error in his calculation of the size of the church is due to his belief that the kingdom will be limited to himself and his following, along with those who repented after hearing the *true* gospel from the Apostles before it was replaced by a "paganized gospel" after the year 69 A.D.

Besides believing and teaching that his is the only *true* gospel preached since 69 A.D., Armstrong also believes that *The World Tomorrow* program was ordained by God Himself to prepare the way for the Lord's return, much in the same manner that John the Baptist was chosen to precede the Savior's first advent. Quoting Isaiah 40:3, where "the Baptist" is described as a voice crying in the wilderness to prepare the way for the Lord, Armstrong explains: "This refers, typically, to John the Baptist, preparing the way before Christ's first coming, more than 1900 years ago. But it refers directly and anti-typically to the VERY PRESENT—when God was going to raise up a people to shout the true Gospel of the now imminent Kingdom of God, worldwide, with a LOUD VOICE (radio-television) preparing the way for His coming as KING to rule all nations!" [10]

For all his accomplishments, Herbert W. Armstrong can only be described as a gifted man. Now in his late seventies, he has been a success as a businessman, evangelist, radio preacher, lecturer, author, editor, and college president. From what can be determined from what we have seen so far of his religious beliefs it can definitely be said that he believes he is the leader of the *true* church today and that he attaches the utmost importance to his work—that of preparing for the *very return* of our Lord. Volume I of his *Autobiography* (containing 510 pages) portrays its author as a man of high moral character, a man of integrity, deeply devoted to his family, free of any objectionable personal habits. Such qualities are commendable. But those persuaded by the Armstrong gospel should take into account that, from the very beginning of the Christian era, there have been religious leaders who, while living exemplary lives, have nonetheless led many into accepting false doctrines. Thus, in spite of evidences of his good character, one should look at Armstrong's claims and his very unorthodox teachings with the greatest care. Such an examination is advised in the Scriptures, in which the Apostle John himself explicitly warns us not to believe every teacher to be a man sent by God, without having put him to the proof. He wrote: "Beloved, believe not every spirit, but try the spirits whether they are of God; because many false prophets are gone out into the world ..." (I John 4:1).

This admonition by John, which is just as timely today as it was in the Apostle's time, is the reason for this work.

CHAPTER II

FOCUS AND FINANCING

To understand the phenomenal growth of Armstrong*ism,* it is necessary to know what attracts the large majority of its converts. With few exceptions, one is first introduced to this sect through *The World Tomorrow* broadcast, which for many years featured the elder Armstrong. The voice of this program now belongs to Garner Ted Armstrong, a son, now about forty. The voice of the younger Armstrong is an appealing one. It has been described by one veteran of the broadcasting industry as one of the "best voices on radio today." It is the kind of voice that is able to make even a dull subject sound interesting, but, as it happens, that is hardly necessary since most of the material used on the broadcast is fascinating enough in itself. These broadcasts, however, contain only an occasional vague hint of the sectarian teachings behind them. Young Armstrong usually discusses, in a fast-moving, matter-of-fact, sometimes sarcastic style, such problems as water and air pollution, race rioting and student rebellions, proper courtship and rules for successful marriage, the population explosion, approaching famines, the dangers of insecticides being used in modern agriculture, and on-the-scene reports from many troubled spots around the world. Perhaps the most interesting of all is their continuing series on certain aspects of nature, such as the "ant," or the "platypus," or the "nematodes," which are truly brilliant studies that shoot holes in the theory of evolution.

As is quite evident from the list just given, this is an entirely different kind of "religious program." Moreover, the listener is impressed that there is no direct appeal for money. Meanwhile, literature, some of it in book size, is offered "ABSOLUTELY FREE." And with the first order of this *free* material also comes the first issue of *The Plain Truth,* also free. Thus, their indoctrination program is begun.

Probably the biggest attraction to Armstrong*ism,* for the many, is Armstrong's millennial teaching which is set forth in his book, *The Wonderful World Tomorrow.* Now the doctrine of a literal thousand-year reign of Christ on this earth, following this present age, is nothing new. Many Scriptures in the Bible describe this reign, during which time, according to Revelation 20:1-3, Satan will be bound and the world will know peace, and the peoples—no longer deceived—will learn to live in the ways of God. Mention of this millennial kingdom is also included in the writings of most of the Early Church Fathers. These early Christian leaders were almost unanimous in giving Revelation 20:4 a literal interpretation. "The Millennium" was also widely taught in the protestant church up through the last century, and several of the well-known evangelicals of today still preach it.

But the average churchgoer these days is usually altogether unfamiliar with Bible teaching on the millennial kingdom, for the simple reason that it is almost never mentioned from the local pulpit which, incidentally, is the place where the average parishioner receives most of his doctrinal training. Yet, innumerable Scriptures speak very plainly of this coming kingdom of God (see Zechariah 14:16-21 for one example), and, Armstrong points out, this is mainly what Jesus came to preach about. Since the established church is not today bringing the world this message, Armstrong argues that it is therefore not the *true* church, but actually pagan, and its ministers, he says, are really false prophets, unknowingly serving Satan, deceiving both themselves and their congregations. However, in his own millennial teaching, Armstrong remains faithful to the

Scriptures only to a certain degree. As we shall see in a later chapter, his *total* concept of this blessed age is very unorthodox.

Also interesting from the newcomer's standpoint is the so-called "British-Israeli theory" taught by Armstrong as an integral part of his indoctrination program. The theory, of course, is nothing new or original, but it is usually the first time that those beginning to follow Armstrong have ever heard of it. This centuries-old legend is promoted by the elder Armstrong in an interesting 226-page book entitled, *The United States and British Commonwealth in Prophecy.*

The hypocrisy in the modern church is also one of Armstrong's favorite themes, and he scores considerable gains with it. He frequently emphasizes that Christ's Church is not many factional denominations full of strife and dissension, but that it is *one* church, its membership united. This is the church he professes to lead. Also, the gospel he and his ministers proclaim, while unorthodox, is dynamic. He is insistent that God's word (as interpreted by himself, of course) should be obeyed one hundred percent rather than the forty percent effort that the established church seems to be saying is entirely sufficient to insure our salvation. From their writings and radio broadcasts it must necessarily be concluded that these people have high moral values, and are sincerely concerned, even urgently concerned, in converting as many as possible to the Armstrong gospel. Fiercely dedicated, they exude a wholesomeness that seems to validate further their claim of being the one *true* church, a claim that they make often, of which the following is an example:

"The true Church—the 'Church of God' (I Cor. 1:2)—is not many divided quarreling denominations, but ONE Church, composed of many scattered members, ONE Church united in Spirit, mind, attitude and heart because its members have totally surrendered their wills to God and have yielded to correction and reproof from the Word of God—the Bible." [1]

Such statements as this one are appealing. It strikes a responsive chord in many thousands who are disillusioned by their own church, which, in many cases, is found "divided" and "quarreling," just as described.

There is also something intriguing about the Armstrong "work." Listeners wonder at its astounding success, from a weekly broadcast over a 100-watt station just thirty-five years ago to a religious organization reaching millions worldwide through radio, magazine and tract publications, while also carrying out its own independent educational program on three college campuses. Such growth, one is first inclined to believe, forgetting for the moment that the heathen religions have shown an even more remarkable growth, must surely have the blessings of God. Just about everyone wonders, too, how this independent religious organization is able to meet its overhead expenses, which are staggering. Consider for a moment, if you will, the costs of the following:

1. Daily broadcasts over more than 377 radio and television stations worldwide.

2. Publishing *The Plain Truth,* with a two-million-plus circulation every month, twelve months out of the year, plus mailing costs, plus maintaining and equipping three printing plants in Pasadena, California, Watford, England, and North Sydney, Australia, and having its "own trained newsmen, news correspondents, contributing editors," and photographers stationed in branch offices throughout the world.

3. Financing the upkeep and providing salaries for the faculties on its three Ambassador College campuses at Pasadena, California, Big Sandy, Texas, and at Bricket Wood, England.

4. The printing and mailing of 80,000 Ambassador College Bible Correspondence Course Lessons each month, plus the millions of other pieces of literature sent out each year, all free and ranging all the way up to book-size.

Such costs add up to a reported annual budget of

thirty-four million dollars. And everyone asks: how in the world do they pay for it? Some indeed become so intrigued by this question that they frequently write in for information, and occasionally mention is made of this curiosity by Armstrong in his personal column in *The Plain Truth,* as in the following example:

"People often ask: 'HOW can you do it? HOW can you publish such a quality magazine of such tremendous circulation worldwide, without advertising revenue, and without subscription price?'

". . .So, since we receive such questions from many subscribers, it seems fitting that the tribute I wish to pay to this small army of volunteers (contributors) should, at the same time, answer that very question.

"When I say you *cannot* pay for your own subscription —it has already been paid—I do so because I do not like to use the word 'FREE.' In the strictest sense nothing is free. That is why we say: 'Your subscription price *has been paid.'* Of course SOMEONE had to pay for it. Yet we never change YOU—the reader. You CANNOT pay for your own. Our mail-opening staff is instructed to return your money if you try.

"This bewilders people. NO ONE ever did anything this way before." [2]

Armstrong goes on to explain that the "SOMEONE" paying for these subscriptions (and, incidentally, all the expenses of the other things as well) are those they call "Co-Workers." These "Co-Workers" are those who have been converted to the Armstrong gospel and tithe their money to him. There are also those of his regular listeners or readers who feel they should send in contributions large enough to pay for the materials they have been receiving free, plus enough to pay for a few others who are probably not able to pay. These latter mentioned, when they have begun to give on a somewhat regular basis, are also elevated to the status of "Co-Worker," and are placed on a special mailing list, even though they perhaps are not Sabbath-keepers, which is necessary if one is to become a *real* Armstrong disciple.

Meanwhile, readers of *The Plain Truth,* numbering perhaps as many as 6,000,000 monthly, plus the 80,000 students taking the Bible Correspondence Course, and an untold number receiving doctrinal pamphlets and books, are told quite often that God's people are commanded to tithe, and if you don't tithe you are stealing from God, and if you think you *are* tithing when giving to a "pagan" church, you really are not, since it's not God's *true* church. The following will illustrate this Armstrong tack:

Tithe to WHICH Church?

"There are over four hundred denominations in the United States alone today. Christ said, 'I will builld My *Church'*—one Church! Mat. 16:18. *He did not say He would build* MANY *churches!* ONLY *ONE* CHURCH—the *one* Church that is preaching the true New Testament gospel of the Kingdom of God of which Jesus is the *living* Head and High Priest—MUST receive your tithes and offerings. Which church?—*God's* Church!

"God's *true* Church must *'teach* all nations' (Mat. 28:19), *'preach* the gospel in all the world for a *witness'* (Mat. 24:14), and *'publish* the gospel among all nations' (Mark 13:10). 'And then shall the end come' (Mat. 24:14). How else can you tell which is His Church? God describes it vividly to you in your Bible so you will not err. *To give to a different church would be WORSE than not giving at all!"*[3]

This of course is a high-powered appeal, much different from the image they portray to the public over the radio where they make it a point to remind their listeners frequently that they don't solicit contributions. These reminders are so frequent, in fact, that they become a kind of negative appeal for funds, and it has truly worked wonders.

CHAPTER III

A BAPTIZED JUDAISM

This book is based upon my own personal experiences as a former Armstrong convert, and I have recited in the preceding chapters incidents about which I had firsthand knowledge. My own involvement in this sect, like most of their converts, began when I became a regular radio listener, then became a Bible correspondence student, a "Co-Worker," and even a "Sabbath-keeper," according to their teachings.

It seems incredible to me now, but, for a fact, I once accepted some of the doctrines which we will examine at length in a moment; others I took as information, not really deciding one way or the other; and there are yet others which I became aware of only later while researching Armstrong's religious background and beliefs.

A thorough study of a great number of their articles dealing with doctrines will reveal some truth, some inconsistencies, some half-truths, and not a few cases of blatant misuse of Scripture. Some of the unorthodox doctrines taught by such sects as Christian Scientists, Seventh Day Adventists, Jehovah's Witnesses and the Mormons have been incorporated into the Armstrong gospel, and he has also borrowed liberally from Judaism, doing away only with circumcision and the ceremonial part of the Mosaic Law, while observing the dietary requirements and the keeping of the Jewish feast days, the Sabbaths, and the like. In many ways, they resemble one of the sects of the Ebionites, a heretical group that went out from the early church. *Ebionite* was the epithet given them, because of the poverty of their understanding of the true doctrines of Christianity. The major difference between the Ebionites and Armstrong*ism* is perhaps the Ebionites' rejection of the epistles of the Apostle Paul. They called him "an apostate from the law." Armstrong accepts these epistles, but spends a great deal of time arguing for a different meaning of certain passages which, if allowed to stand as they have been traditionally interpreted, without challenge, would disprove certain of his long-held tenets. He is clearly more at home with the Old Testament where his Judaic teachings are not only *not* disputed, but are given scriptural backing. For want of a better word, his religion might be described as a "baptized Judaism."

Nearly all of his doctrinal errors have to do with the New Testament. This is a personal opinion, and should be so regarded, but in studying the history of this movement, along with their writings over a period of several years, it seemed to me that Armstrong often "got the cart before the horse," that is, he formulated doctrines based on his own personal whims or upon certain Scriptures that he comprehended out of context, and then found it necessary to prove. One might surmise that he had already reaped a good measure of success before he began to be confronted by listeners and readers with Scriptures that plainly contradicted certain of his teachings. To admit error, however, would have been to confess that his was not, after all, the *true* church, and this, in turn, would probably have meant the loss of his fairly large following which was supplying the money for the "work." it is evident in some cases that where he could not avoid it, and where the point was not really all that important anyway, he temporized. But where it concerned his more firmly established doctrines, he seemed to have been both unable and unwilling to accept correction. Thus, it became necessary to compromise the Scriptures that stood in the way of his religion. Several examples of this will be clearly seen in the following chapters.

CHAPTER IV

PREPARING THE NEW CONVERT

Jesus said:

34 — Think not that I am come to send peace on earth: I came not to send peace, but a sword.

35 — For I am come to set a man at variance against his father, and the daughter against her mother, and the daughter-in-law against her mother-in-law.

36 — And a man's foes shall be they of his own household.

The above statement is from Matthew, chapter ten. What does it mean? It plainly says that those of a man's household who are not Christian will naturally be at variance with those who profess Christ. But the word "variance," having a wide range of meaning, can be defined as anything from a mild difference of opinion to an outright dispute. And "foe" can designate anyone from a hated enemy to only "one who opposes." But which of these definitions did Jesus Himself attach to His words? And what are we to understand from them? In other words, what do these few but difficult verses really teach?

They teach, states *Adam Clarke's Commentary,* that the "spirit of Christ can have no union with the spirit of the world. Even a father, while unconverted, will oppose a godly child. Thus the spirit that is in those who sin against God is opposed to that spirit which is in the followers of the Most High."

But *The Abingdon Bible Commentary* gives these three verses this sense: "Jesus intimates that what he had experienced in his own home would be a common experience wherever his message was proclaimed." (See Mark 3:21, 31-35; 6:1-6.)

Matthew Henry's Commentary perhaps comes closest in capturing Jesus' intended meaning. The terms, says Henry, for being a Christian are that we must prefer Christ "before our nearest and dearest relations: *father or mother, son or daughter.* Children must love their parents, and parents must love their children; but if they love them better than Christ, they are unworthy of him. As we must not be *deterred* from Christ by the hatred of our relations which he spoke of (v. 21, 35, 36), so we must not be *drawn* from him, by their love."*

Armstrong, along with some others, has placed an entirely different meaning upon this particular passage. Declaring that his followers compose the only *true* Church of God, and are therefore the only *true* Christians, and that all others professing themselves to be Christians are actually pagans, he tells those just beginning to follow after him to expect trouble and persecution from both family and former friends, and he suggests to them that they "must discontinue their relationships with this sinning society," that is, *all* those who do not belong to the Armstrong cult.[1] In this manner they prepare the new disciple against allowing his commitment to the Armstrong gospel to be affected in any way by family ties. It is used quite frequently in their indoctrination program. The following is but one example:

"Did you know Jesus Christ Himself said—IF YOU ARE A TRUE CHRISTIAN, YOUR FORMER FRIENDS, YOUR RELATIVES, THIS SOCIETY—WILL HATE YOU?

"...Jesus said *your own family* would begin to look down on you, if you are really willing to OBEY HIM!

"...If you are really following Christ—LIVING as He lived, DOING as He did—keeping God's LAW as He did—this society, even your closest former friends and your own relatives, will begin to RESIST and

PERSECUTE you." [2]

The reader is then told that it is God's will for *true* Christians "that they must discontinue their relationships with this sinning society!"[3]

These statements, as is quite obvious, reveal a definite tendency toward monasticism, which, to a certain extent, is practiced by the hard-core Armstrong following. They do not, of course, like some monastics, withdraw entirely, but they eschew involvement as much as possible in this "sinning society." Instead, they devote themselves to their religion, while awaiting for the return of Christ who, they say, is the only One who can solve the world's problems. Orthodox Christianity also teaches that it will take such a government, established by Christ, to bring a lasting peace and justice among mankind; but in the meantime, is it God's will that His people keep themselves separate? Is this taught in the Bible?

Actually the exact opposite is true.

Rather than withdrawal, the Christian is called upon to undertake a life of positive personal witness, to follow the examples set by the apostles. Had these New Testament Christians adopted such a policy, the establishing of Christ's Church would have been seriously hampered. This danger of withdrawal was quite evident to Paul, and his instructions to the Corinthians on this very point were most explicit. Some of this church, having misunderstood something that the Apostle had written them in previous correspondence, had apparently lapsed into the practice of monasticism. This brought a quick response from Paul. To make certain they did not continue in this error, he sent the Corinthians this clarification:

> "I wrote to you in my letter not to associate with immoral men; NOT AT ALL MEANING THE IMMORAL OF THIS WORLD,* or the greedy and robbers, or idolaters, since then you would need to go out of the world. But rather I wrote to you NOT TO ASSOCIATE with any one who bears the name of

brother if he is guilty of immorality or greed, or is an idolater, reviler, drunkard, or robber—not even to eat with such a one." (I Corinthians 5:9-11 RSV)

We should, then, CONTINUE (not "discontinue") our association with the immoral, the greedy, the robbers, and even the idolaters of this present age. To these the Christian gives his witness, hoping to save some from "the fire" (Jude 23). And if we are faithful to Paul's instructions, we will have nothing *at all* to do with one who, after being baptized into the Christian faith, blasphemes the Name by returning to his old ways.

Now, in regards to their teaching that the new convert must expect to be persecuted and hated by members of his or her own family, this sect knows—after many years of experience—that their highly unorthodox doctrines are bound to cause trouble in the family, especially if other members of the family happen to be active in the orthodox Christian church. Thus, well in advance, the proselyte is prepared for this eventuality. He is even led to believe that when the new doctrines he has accepted are called into serious question by the family that his resistance really proves whether or not he is truly "following Christ— LIVING as He lived, DOING as He did—keeping God's LAW as He did."

Their position on this is challenged by Paul. The Apostle taught that there should be peace in the family, even if it is made up of believers and unbelievers. And, he told the Corinthians, the family should remain together unless the unbeliever chooses to depart. His instructions on this are contained in the following passage: "But to the rest speak I, not the Lord: If any brother hath a wife that believeth not, and she be pleased to dwell with him, let him NOT PUT HER AWAY. And the woman which hath an husband that believeth not, and if he be pleased to dwell with her, LET HER NOT LEAVE HIM. For the unbelieving husband is sanctified by the wife, and the unbelieving wife is sanctified by the husband: else were your children unclean; but now are they holy. BUT IF THE UNBELIEVING DEPART, LET HIM DEPART. A brother or a sister is not under bondage in such cases: BUT GOD HATH CALLED US TO PEACE." (I Corinthians 7:12-15 RSV)

CHAPTER V

EARLY CHURCH WRITINGS
DISCOUNTED

Very early in their indoctrination program, the idea is gotten across to their new converts that most of the writings which have come down to us from the early church are not to be trusted. These letters and treatises, which give us invaluable insights into the religious practices of the early Christians, are thus shunned by most of their proselytes as the work of false brethren doing Satan's will. The church they represented, Armstrong teaches, was clearly already corrupted. This subversion, the students are told, began as early as 33 A.D., with the appearance of one Simon Magus of Samaria (see Acts 8:9-24). The truth continued to be preached, but only for a few more years, when it was replaced, says Armstrong, by false, pagan doctrines. The gospel of Christ, he most emphatically declares, "was not preached to the world after 69 A.D." [1]

Armstrong's attempts to discredit the early church writings are completely understandable. There are certain statements made in these ancient letters concerning such things as the observance of the Lord's day, the Trinity, a regular Eucharist, and the abrogation of the Mosaic Law that are not at all compatible with Armstrong's teachings. These writings which we speak of—by Ignatius, Irenaeus, Justin Martyr, Clement, Barnabas, and others—are really an embarrassment to him, and, of course, he had little choice but to categorically deny that these early church leaders were *true* Christians. Yet, three of the five named here eventually were martyred, thus giving the ultimate testimony of their faith.

It is true, as Armstrong charges, that false brethren did *eventually* succeed in joining themselves to the church. Jesus Himself predicted this would happen, describing these as "ravening wolves" presenting themselves "in sheep's clothing" (Matthew 7:15). So warned the apostles also. Paul underscored this threat to the physical church in his farewell speech to the elders of the church at Ephesus before his final journey to Jerusalem. He told the Ephesians: "Take heed, therefore, unto yourselves, and to all the flock, over which the Holy Spirit hath made you overseers, to feed the church of God, which he hath purchased with his own blood. For I know this, that after my departing shall grievous wolves enter in among you, not sparing the flock" (Acts 20:28-29 Scofield Bible).

And this happened—but not as Armstrong maintains. Not even the physical church was despoiled as early as he would have you to believe. Nor was the true gospel all at once cut off in 69 A.D., and never heard again until Armstrong's first broadcast in 1934. The subverting of the *physical* church was a gradual process, not something which occurred suddenly, overnight. And it was not even successful in a true sense, for the *true* church, that is, the *spiritual* church, which is The Church within the physical church, has never even been touched by Satan. Indeed, it cannot be, for Christ Himself declared that the very "gates of hell shall not prevail against it" (Matthew 16:18).

No student of early church history can accept Armstrong's cutoff date of 69 A.D. (or 67 A.D., as he has stated in other places). In this, the martyrs of the first three centuries, and the blood they shed, are evidence against him. One has only to read the accounts of their sufferings unto death in such works as Eusebius' *Ecclesiastical History* or W.H.C. Frend's *Martyrdom and Persecution in the Early Church* or Philip Schaff's *History of the Christian Church* to be fully and completely convinced of the validity of their faith. During these persecutions, the provincial Roman rulers tried to outdo one another in devising the cruelest of tortures. Burnings at the stake or being tossed to wild beasts in the arena were merciful sentences compared to some of the methods of execution employed, one of which was to place the Christian in an "iron chair" and suspend him over the flames to allow him to smell his own flesh as he was slowly roasted to death. And yet all the prisoner had to do to escape such horrible punishment and death was simply to deny the Name of Christ and partake of food sacrificed to idols or to burn incense to the gods—an opportunity that was, with a few possible exceptions, offered to each and every accused Christian who appeared before the provincial governors. What could possibly exceed such a testimony?

Just as Christ prophesied of the danger of "false prophets," so also He foretold that many would be *delivered up and put to death* "for my name's sake" (Matthew 24:9). Yet, according to Armstrong's gospel, martyrs could not really have been *true* Christians, for the world had not the *true* gospel preached to them after 69 A.D., until nearly nineteen centuries later.

CHAPTER VI

THE CHRISTIAN AND THE MOSAIC LAW

Is the Mosaic Law, which the children of Israel accepted in a covenant made with the Lord at Mount Sinai (Ex. 19:8), and which was administered under the Levitical priesthood, also binding upon the Christian? In other words, is the Christian "under the Law"?

Or, since the priesthood of the Levites was changed, with Jesus becoming our High Priest, was the Law also changed, providing the Christian with a far better covenant?

These are two opposing views—or ways. One is *The Way*. The other is *a way*. One is false. The other leads to salvation.

They are not reconcilable.

The latter view, which is the traditional evangelical teaching, is vigorously opposed by the Armstrong cult. They say that the Christian is still very much under (or "within") the Law given at Mount Sinai. They acknowledge only that the ceremonial part of the Law, including the service of the Levitical priesthood, has been done away with. They claim that these ceremonial observances were what Paul spoke of as having been *nailed to the cross* (Col. 2:11-15). In words to this effect, they believe that our relationship to God is still based on the legalistic observance of the Ten Commandments and other aspects of the Mosaic Law, including the keeping of the Sabbath (Saturday), and the Jewish holy days as set forth in Leviticus 23.

While the Law is their guide to salvation, they do not like to be regarded as "under the law," however. They prefer the phrase "within the law," which they use frequently and go to some lengths to explain. Between the two they make this distinction: "To obey the law is to be 'within the law.' To sin—disobey—is to become 'under the law!' "[1] Thus, those who sin are "under the law." Those that do *not* sin are "within the law." The Armstrong people say they are "within the law."

Most orthodox Christians, however, maintain that it was this very type of legalistic observance which produced the hypocrites of Christ's own day. In order that the church He bought with His own blood might avoid this error, Christ gave to His people "a much better covenant," whereby we are now under grace.

Orthodox believers point out that in the Law handed down by Moses, God *demanded* obedience and love. Needless to say, love that is demanded is both imperfect and inferior. Similarly, a relationship that is based on fear, as was evident among the Hebrews at Mount Sinai, is certainly not conducive to a perfect love, neither can it be. In other words, love cannot be perfect unless fear is first taken out of the way. "There is no fear in love," wrote the Apostle John on this very point; "but perfect love casts out fear" (I John 4:18 RSV). This change in God's relationship to men was clearly signified, say the orthodox, by the following statement by Jesus to His disciples: "Henceforth I call you NOT SERVANTS; for the servant knoweth not what his lord doeth: but I HAVE CALLED YOU FRIENDS. . ." (John 15:15). These words of Christ are of tremendous importance. This change from the role of SERVANT, as under the Mosaic Law, to FRIENDS, whereby we have fellowship with Him, has been called the very "genius of the Christian faith."

It was upon this very principle that the Apostle Paul boldly asserted, in numerous passages, that the Law of Moses had been superseded by a much better covenant, which in I Corinthians 9:21 and Galatians 6:2 he calls "the law of Christ." This is what he meant when he penned the following to the Christians at Rome: "But now we are discharged FROM THE LAW, dead to that which held us captive, so that WE SERVE NOT UNDER THE OLD WRITTEN CODE but in the NEW LIFE OF THE SPIRIT" (Romans 7:6 RSV). What Paul is saying here is that, instead of the Law of Moses being our guide, we *now* have the Holy Spirit to lead us (II Corinthians 3:6-8).

Armstrong has succeeded in causing many to be confused on this point. Evidently he is confused himself. But there is really nothing difficult about it. All one has to do is believe Paul when he says: "For sin will have no dominion over you, since YOU ARE NOT UNDER LAW BUT UNDER GRACE" (Romans 6:14 RSV).

This is a simple statement.

No one could possibly fail to understand its meaning unless he deliberately chose to do so, or else is spiritually blinded to it. Paul says that Christians ARE NOT UNDER THE LAW. To say that Christians are "under the law" or "within the law" is to call Paul a liar. Does this mean that the Ten Commandments, as a system, are not in effect? No. These commandments and their penalties still hang over everyone who is not a true Christian, all who are not led by the Spirit (Gal. 5:18). This includes not only the Jews and the Gentile nonbelievers, but also all those who claim to be Christians who willingly place themselves under it, or "within it."

Armstrong's biggest difficulty with the Law is his belief that it is eternal, as a system. (But if this be true, what place will such commandments as "Thou shalt not commit adultery" have in the Kingdom of God, where His people neither marry nor are given in marriage; and "Thou shalt not murder," in a place where life is eternal?)

Opposed to this is the orthodox school which believes that the Mosaic Law as a system was of a temporary nature which "was our custodian until Christ came, that we might be justified by faith" (Galatians 3:24 RSV). This was Paul's view. For him the Law of Moses "was a revelation which came at one particular time in history—that is, there was a period of time in history before it was given—and it could therefore be supplanted by a revelation more recent in history. Moreover, the Law of Moses was in Paul's mind not a direct echo of God. Of its origin, he tells us that it was 'ordained by angels through an intermediary' (Gal. 3:19; see also Acts 7:53, and Hebrews 2:2)." [2]

Concerning this Pauline doctrine, Samuel Sandmel has written: "Rabbinic Judaism assumed that the ancient revelation of Law required the subsequent age to be faithful to the revelation by applying its principles and its details to every conceivable situation. Paul, on the other hand, saw the ancient revelation to Moses not as a crucial, decisive event, but as a single milestone in a long road of revelations, whose climax came in Paul's own time. For the rabbis, the climax was in Moses, and Sinai to them was the highest mountain; for Paul, Sinai was only a hill, which had now sunk below the horizon ... The rabbis said: God's greatest revelation in the past obligates you to observe His laws; Paul said: Moses revealed a pretty good Law, but there had been a revelation of God to Abraham better and earlier than to Moses, and a revelation in Christ Jesus better and later than to Moses, and Moses' Law is no longer binding ..." [3]

This change in the law is set forth in numerous Scriptures, but nowhere is it made plainer than in the Epistle to the Hebrews, where the author, addressing Jewish converts to the Christian faith, explains: "Now if perfection had been attainable through the Levitical priesthood (for under it the people received the law), what further need would there have been for another priest to arise after the order of Melchizedek, rather than one named after the order of Aaron? For when there is a CHANGE IN THE PRIESTHOOD, there is NECESSARILY A CHANGE IN THE LAW as well" (Hebrews 7:11-12 RSV).

But what is this new "Law of Christ," which Paul speaks about, and how does it differ from the old Mosaic Law which was delivered to the Hebrews? Explains the *New*

Scofield Reference Bible: "The new law of Christ is the divine love, as wrought into the renewed heart by the Holy Spirit (Rom. 5:5; Heb. 10:16), which flows out in the energy of the Spirit, unforced and spontaneous, toward the objects of the divine love (2 Cor. 5:14-20; 1 Th. 2:7-8). It is, therefore, 'the law of liberty' (Jas. 1:25, 2:12) in contrast with the external law of Moses. Moses' law demands love (Lev. 19:18, Dt. 6:5; Luke 10:27); Christ's law is love (Rom. 5:5, 1 Jn. 4:7, 19-20), and so takes the place of the external law by fulfilling it (Rom. 13:10; Gal. 5:14). It is the 'law written in the heart' under the New Covenant (see Heb. 8:8. . .)." [4]

In Paul's view, these two systems, that is, the Mosaic Law and the "Law of Christ," cannot coexist in the believer. He declares, "You are severed from Christ, you who would be justified by the law; you have fallen away from grace" (Galatians 5:4 RSV).

The real significance of the difference between the "Law of Christ" and the Mosaic Law might be more readily seen and understood in this allegory related by Paul in chapter four of Galatians (Scofield Bible):

19 — My little children, of whom I travail in birth again until Christ be formed in you,

20 — I desire to be present with you now, and to change my tone; for I STAND IN DOUBT OF YOU.

21 — Tell me, ye that desire to be under the law, do ye not hear the law?

22 — For it is written that Abraham had two sons, the one by a bondmaid, the other by a freewoman.

23 — But he who was of the bondwoman was born after the flesh; but he of the freewoman was by promise;

24 — Which things are an allegory; for THESE ARE THE TWO COVENANTS: the one from the MOUNT SINAI, bearing children for bondage, who is Hagar.

25 — For this Hagar is MOUNT SINAI in Arabia, and answereth to Jerusalem which now is, and is in bondage with her children.

26 — But Jerusalem which is above is free, which is

the mother of us all.

27 — For it is written, Rejoice, thou barren that bearest not; break forth and cry, thou that travailest not; for the desolate hath many more children than she who hath an husband.

28 — Now we, brethren, as Isaac was, ARE THE CHILDREN OF PROMISE.

29 — But as then he that was born after the flesh persecuted him that was born after the Spirit, even so it is now.

30 — Nevertheless, what saith the scripture? Cast out the bondwoman and her son; for the son of the bondwoman shall not be heir with the son of the freewoman.

31 — So then, brethren, WE ARE NOT CHIL-DREN of the BONDWOMAN, but of the FREE [margin] WOMAN.

Now the lesson that Paul draws for us here is clear. We, he says, meaning those of the *true* Christian faith, are not children of Mount Sinai, where the Mosaic Law was given. Those, he plainly declares, are in bondage. On the other hand, Christians, like Isaac who lived long before the Law was given, are "the children of promise." By his teachings, Armstrong and the ministers who carry his gospel have placed untold thousands in bondage to Mount Sinai.

In his booklet, *Dead to the Law,* the late M.R. DeHaan, writer, medical doctor, Christian minister, and founder of the *Radio Bible Class,* has presented a very vivid picture of the meaning of the "Law of Christ," and shows how it has superseded the law given at Mount Sinai. Since so much depends upon a correct understanding of this doctrine, we have quoted from his work at length:

"The Christian is not under the law according to Scripture. In the eyes of the law he is a dead man. As a member of the Body of Christ by faith he died in the Body of Christ on Calvary. He was buried, raised and today is positionally already seated on the right hand of God. But while he is dead to the law, we are not without law, or lawless. The charge that we who preach grace and freedom from the law teach that we now have a license to live in sin and iniquity and to live for self, reveals a total ignorance of the truth of God's grace. The Christian, free from the law of commandments, is now under a much higher law, the law of love. His motive for service is love and gratitude and thankfulness for so great a salvation, and love itself is the fulfillment of the law.

"The law could not make us better. It could only show us how bad we were. It could not make us holy; it could only reveal our unholiness. The law is just and perfect and holy, and because it is just, it demanded the death of the unjust. Because it is perfect, it condemned our imperfection. Because it is holy, it had to punish our sin. Our hope lies alone in Christ, both to be saved and to be kept, for that which the law could not do, Jesus did for us. Now we serve God through grace and love, our service to Him is motivated only by love, and never by fear.

CHRIST IN US

"Paul therefore says not only, 'I am dead to the law,' but adds also, 'but alive unto God.' And then he elaborates in the next verse in Galatians 2:20, and says this:

> 'I am crucified with Christ: nevertheless I live; yet not I, but Christ liveth in me: and the life which I now live in the flesh I live by the faith [notice, not by the law, but by the FAITH] of the Son of God, who loved me, and gave Himself for me.'

"Paul is now under a new law, the law of love and the law of a new life. The old law of commandments was the law of sin and of death, and Paul says 'that law slew me.' But now, being made free from the law, I live the life of Christ. 'Christ liveth in me.' My motive for holiness is not any more the fear of the law or judgment, but the love of Christ. The Christian under grace serves God because of gratitude and thankfulness for a free and full salvation. He serves God, not through fear, but by love, for 'perfect love casteth out all fear.'

"Oh, how often I pity those poor, professing Christians

who serve God and behave themselves because of the fear of God's judgment or of His chastening. How we pity those poor souls who serve God and abstain from this thing and that thing, and observe this commandment and that commandment, this day instead of that day, because they fear that they may lose their salvation if they do not do it. Let me repeat that. My heart goes out to those poor souls who must hold themselves in bondage because they fear if they do this or that, they will again be lost. That is not the service which God wants, or is pleased with in our lives. He wants a service born of gratitude and love and devotion. I don't want my children to obey me because they fear the punishment they will receive if they are disobedient. I want them to obey me and do all they can for me because of their love for me, and out of devotion and gratitude for that which I have done, am doing, and which they know I will do for them. Now God too wants a loving, joyful service in the same way, not the service of coercion or the threatening of judgment.

AN ILLUSTRATION

"Allow me to illustrate this for you. I am away from home quite frequently and Mrs. De Haan remains at home to look after things while I am gone. Now do you suppose I put her under laws and regulations when I leave? Imagine for a moment that I am about to leave my home, and before I go I put up a great big sign, several feet square, in the kitchen where it is very prominent. Then when I am ready to go away, I call my wife and say, 'Now, Mrs. De Haan, listen to me, your boss. You see those rules up there. There are ten of them. They are your ten commandments by which you are to live in this home.' And then follow the commandments:

Commandment No. 1. Thou shalt entertain no other husband besides me.

Commandment No. 2. Thou shalt not run around gadding

or love anyone else more than me.

Commandment No. 3. Thou shalt not speak lightly or disparagingly about me, your husband, or take my name in vain.

Commandment No. 4. Thou shalt properly clothe and feed my children, and not allow them to starve.

Commandment No. 5. Thou shalt keep the house clean, and not sweep the dust under the rug.

"And so on, and so on, I could go through the whole ten commandments, and I warn her and say, 'Failure to observe these rules will be severely punished by me, your husband. I may even divorce you.'

"Now do you think that I need that kind of a sign for my wife in my home? Do I have to lay down one single law? I should say not! And why not? Simply because she loves me. She is under the law of love. She loves her home, she loves her children, she delights in doing things for us, because she loves us. And so I have no laws tacked up in our kitchen, but when I get ready to leave, we kneel together in prayer, I give her a good hug and a real big kiss, and I am off, with never a care or a worry about my home, or the conduct of Mrs. De Haan.

SERVANTS NEED LAWS

"Now if my wife were a servant or a slave or working for wages, then of course we would need laws and rules. We would need a contract and an understanding about what her duties were, what the wages would be, and a hundred other commandments. But not so with us. We are in love, more madly in love today than we were thirty-six years ago when we were married. You see, the more love, the less law. The less love, the more law. In our home we have no law but love. And if you are a true believer, you too are dead to the law, and now live by grace and love unto God. If you are still alive to sin and self, then, indeed, the law still threatens you.

"In this connection consider with me carefully Romans 7. After having shown in Romans 6 that we are dead to the law and alive unto God, Paul then gives a very striking illustration. It is quite a long passage, but I feel that I must read it all and I trust you will bear with me. Listen carefully, God is speaking through Paul in the 7th chapter of Romans, beginning with verse 1, and says:

'Know ye not, brethren, (for I speak to them that know the law,) how that the law hath dominion over a man as long as he liveth?

For the woman which hath an husband is bound by the law to her husband so long as he liveth: but if the husband be dead, she is loosed from the law of her husband.

So then if, while her husband liveth, she be married to another man, she shall be called an adulteress: but if her husband be dead, she is free from that law; so that she is no adulteress, though she be married to another man.

Wherefore, my brethren, ye also are become dead to the law by the body of Christ; that ye should be married to another, even to him who is raised from the dead, that we should bring forth fruit unto God.

For when we were in the flesh, the motions of sins, which were by the law, did work in our members to bring forth fruit unto death.

But now we are delivered from the law, that being dead wherein we were held; that we should serve in newness of spirit, and not in the oldness of the letter.'

"Certainly, comment on these verses seems almost superfluous. Yet, it is such a convincing truth that we must emphasize one or two points here. This is a double-barreled passage, for it not only illustrates our freedom from the law but uses the illustration of a husband and wife and gives us just another inkling of the Bible teaching on the matter of remarriage of divorced persons. Let me repeat verses 2 and 3:

'For the woman which hath an husband is bound by the law to her husband so long as he liveth: but if the husband be dead, she is loosed from the law of her husband.

So then if, while her husband liveth, she be married to another man, she shall be called an adulteress: but if her husband be dead, she is free from the law; so that she is no adulteress, though she be married to another man.'

"Now here is a plain, inescapable, and unmistakable statement, that no one, speaking of course about believers, is ever to remarry while the first mate is still alive. But that, of course, is a side issue. We are dealing now with our relationship to the law, and the case of the husband and wife is introduced merely as an illustration, and yet it sets forth God's Word in regard to this matter just the same.

"A woman is bound by the law to her husband so long as he liveth, but if the husband be dead, she is loosed from the law of her husband. If she is joined with another while the husband still lives, it constitutes adultery. Only death can dissolve the legal relationship. Even so, for believers, says Paul, who profess to be married to Christ and then still cling to the law, they too are guilty of spiritual adultery. How convincing the words, therefore:

'Wherefore, my brethren, ye also are become dead to the law by the body of Christ; that ye should be married to another, even to him who is raised from the dead, that we should bring forth fruit unto God.'

"Now I do trust that this will further help you to understand the words which we have taken for our subject in all this series of messages,

'For I through the law am dead to the law, that I might live unto God.' (Gal. 2:19)

"Now, I realize very keenly that this truth is hard to receive, for it means death to pride, and self, and the flesh. Grace, the truth of grace, means death to all fleshly pride. It is so pleasing to our flesh to feel that somehow we do have a little bit to do with earning our own salvation, either earning it or keeping it. It is a tremendously humbling truth to accept, that we are so hopelessly lost by sin that God must do it all and we can do nothing at all to help. But I hear someone say, 'That is partly true. I believe, too, that we are justified by faith, but after we are saved, then we must be kept by our own works and the keeping of the law, mustn't we?' Oh, my friend, do you really mean that? Do you really believe that a man ever lived (except Jesus), who ever kept the law of God perfectly in every detail and continuously? Remember, to hate your brother is to be a murderer. To covet is to be a thief. To look upon a woman, according to Jesus, to lust after her is the same as committing adultery. Remember, the very thought of foolishness is sin according to Proverbs 24:9. An idle word, according to Christ, is sin. And the law demands perfection. It is not enough to try to do your best. To transgress one commandment is to be guilty of all. Now let me ask you, can any man stand that test? Then why should anyone claim to be saved by grace and then kept by the works of the law? We may best answer it in the words of Paul in Galatians, chapter 3. Remember that these Galatian Christians professed to have been saved by grace, justified by faith alone, and then after they were saved, they were putting themselves back again under the works of the law, and Paul says to them:

> *'O foolish Galatians, who hath bewitched you, that ye should not obey the truth, before whose eyes Jesus Christ hath been evidently set forth, crucified among you?*
>
> *This only would I learn of you, Received ye the Spirit by the works of the law, or by the hearing of faith?*
>
> *Are ye so foolish? having begun in the Spirit, are ye now made perfect by the flesh?*
>
> *Have ye suffered so many things in vain? if it be yet in vain.*
>
> *He therefore that ministereth to you the Spirit, and worketh miracles among you, doeth he it by the works of the law, or by the hearing of faith?* (Gal. 3:1-5)

"From this it should be perfectly evident, my friend, that the law can neither save you, keep you, nor make you better. Paul says, in Romans 8:3,

> *'For what the law could not do, in that it was weak through the flesh, God sending his own Son in the likeness of sinful flesh, and for sin, condemned sin in the flesh:*
>
> *That the righteousness of the law might be fulfilled in us, who walk not after the flesh, but after the Spirit.'* (Romans 8:3-4)

"The law cannot save, the law cannot keep. It is only Christ who is able to do that. The law was given by God to prove once and for all that man could not save himself by works. It was given to show the utter depravity of the flesh and of human nature, to cause us to flee to Christ for mercy, not for justice, but for mercy; for forgiveness, not condemnation; for grace, and not our just deserts." [5]

CHAPTER VII

THE CHRISTIAN AND THE SABBATH

Not unlike Judaism on this point, Armstrong*ism* teaches the proselyte not to love God but to fear Him, much in the same manner as the Hebrews were taught at Mount Sinai. Fear is woven into their doctrines at every place possible. It abounds everywhere in their writings. It is spoken continuously in the hearers' ears, incessantly, without letup. Thus instilled, fear becomes a part of the makeup of the Armstrong convert.

The Armstrong ministers and writers are not amateurs. Like master propagandists, they know how to play on this emotion. For an example, take their teaching on the Fourth Commandment. They constantly hammer at the disciple, both new and old, that this is the "identifying SIGN" between God and His people "forever." It is also the "test" commandment for proving obedience to God. And only by keeping the Sabbath, they say, can a person have "a right relationship with the *true* God."[1] Their technique is further illustrated by the following warnings given by Roderick C. Meredith to all the Armstrong faithful:

"The beginning of all truth is to FEAR God (Pro. 1:7). You who understand should *fear* to break the fourth commandment and thus violate God's Sabbath day!

"God calls the Sabbath: 'My holy day' (Isa. 58:13). The Creator Himself has sanctified and set apart this period of time in which to *rest* and *worship* Him. If you appropriate this day for your own business or pleasure, you are STEALING from God—and you are guilty as a thief and a violator of the eighth commandment! You are also 'coveting' time that *does not belong to you,* but to God, and are therefore *breaking* the tenth commandment also! You are certainly putting something ahead of the true God, and are therefore reckoned as GUILTY of breaking the first commandment! You are breaking the fifth commandment as well, for you are *dishonoring* and *disobeying* your spiritual Father in Heaven!" [2]

It is fact that the keeping of the Sabbath was to be a "sign" between God and the Hebrew people, and it has been so from the time to Moses down to this very day. The Jews, who are the only people who know for a certainty they are descended from Israel, still keep the seventh day, in all the lands in which they have been scattered. But the pact made at Mount Sinai was between God and the Israelites. That pact was ratified by the Hebrew elders (see Deuteronomy 29:10-15). It was meant for the Hebrew people. But Armstrong and his ministers insist that Christians today are just as bound by this "sign" as were the Hebrews because Christians are "spiritual Israelites." [3]

If Armstrong is correct in this view, then we who claim to be true Christians should be willing to take correction and keep the Sabbath. To do otherwise, if he is correct, is to stand guilty of his charge that we are false brethren, deceived by Satan. But is he correct?

According to all available evidence, which includes New Testament Scriptures, the very earliest ecclesiastical writings, and at least one letter written by a Roman official, the Christian Church from the earliest times has observed the first day of the week (Sunday) as the Lord's day.

But this church, argues Armstrong, was not the *true* Christian Church, but was the one that was subverted early (about 69 A.D.) by false brethren who "crept in unawares—deceiving people—TURNING GRACE INTO LICENSE!" [4] The *true* church, he declares, has always observed the seventh day, that is, the Jewish Sabbath, which is commanded the Hebrews in the Old Testament.

Saturday, he also claims, was the day Christ arose from the dead—not Sunday as has long been supposed.

Moreover (and this will come as a shock to many listeners and "Co-Workers" who have not been fully initiated into the religion of this cult), Armstrong teaches that all those who commemorate Christ's resurrection on the first day of the week (Sunday) shall have the "mark of the beast," which is mentioned in the Revelation of John. In fact, he says, *this is* the "mark of the beast." He charges that those who honor this stated day will be the ones "tormented with fire and brimstone" (see Revelation 14:9-10), a torment which the Bible says will last "for ever and ever."* As incredible as this may sound to many, this is their conviction, their actual teaching, and they, along with their hard-core followers, apparently believe it with every ounce of their being. This Armstrong doctrine is set forth in a booklet entitled, *The Mark of the Beast.* (See also *Which Day Is the Sabbath?* p.3.)

Armstrong has won many converts to Sabbath-keeping because he is able to point to the Fourth Commandment of the Mosaic Law, and insist that the true church must obey it.

Meanwhile, those who do keep the Lord's day have no specific Bible command to do so, but base their commemoration of it as the day of Christ's victory over death and the grave. That this observance goes all the way back to the earliest Christians, Philip Schaff, a recognized authority on church history in the last century, had no doubt. In his monumental eight-volume work which is still widely used, Schaff said: "The celebration of the Lord's Day in memory of the resurrection of Christ dates undoubtedly from the apostolic age. Nothing short of apostolic precedent can account for the universal religious observance in the churches of the second century. There is no dissenting voice. This custom is confirmed by the testimonies of the earliest post-apostolic writers, as Barnabas, Ignatius, and

Justin Martyr. It is also confirmed by the younger Pliny. The *Didache* calls the first day 'the Lord's Day of the Lord.' "[5]

Furthermore, Schaff declared: "the fathers did not regard the Christian Sunday as a continuation of, but as a substitute for, the Jewish Sabbath, and based it not so much on the fourth commandment, and the primitive rest of God in creation, to which the commandment expressly refers, as upon the resurrection of Christ and the apostolic tradition. There was a disposition to disparage the Jewish law in the zeal to prove the independent originality of Christian institutions . . . Sunday was always regarded in the ancient church as a divine institution, at least in the secondary sense, as distinct from divine ordinances in the primary sense, which were directly and positively commanded by Christ, as baptism and the Lord's Supper. Regular public worship absolutely requires a stated day of worship." [6]

In addition to "the apostolic tradition" and the early writings, a few of which are mentioned by Schaff, those who honor the first day of the week as the day of Christ's resurrection point to Mark 16:9 as the scriptural basis for their conclusion. Here it is written:

> Now when Jesus had risen early on the first day of the week, he appeared first to Mary Magdalene, out of whom he had cast seven devils.

As it stands, this is a positive statement that Christ arose on the first day of the week. And this is the sense given to this verse by all translators. However, in the Greek originals of the New Testament writings, there were no punctuation marks or punctuation indicators, not even spaces between words, which were all written in capital letters. This being the case, Armstrong has taken the liberty to move one of the commas. Thus we have:

> Now when Jesus had risen, early on the first day of the week he appeared first to Mary Magdalene, out of whom he had cast seven devils.

With this "correction," the verse, obviously no longer states positively that the resurrection of Christ took place on Sunday. It still could have. Or it could have occurred earlier—on the Sabbath. This is the day Armstrong teaches his disciples that Christ arose. Moreover, he has been able to convince his following that he is right.

However, there is another passage that has been overlooked by Armstrong, and perhaps others also, which establishes that the resurrection occurred on the first day of the week, just as it is stated in Mark 16:9. This verification is found in Luke 24. Here it is recorded that ON THE FIRST DAY OF THE WEEK Mary Magdalene, Joanna, Mary, the mother of James, "and certain others" went to the tomb, "taking spices which they had prepared," but they found the stone rolled away and the tomb empty. This news was immediately reported to the apostles by the women upon their return. Peter had run to the tomb to verify it. Luke continues with the following account:

> 13 — And, behold two of them went THAT SAME DAY to a village called Emmaus, which was from Jerusalem about threescore furlongs.
>
> 14 — And they talked together of all these things which had happened.
>
> 15 — And it came to pass that, while they communed together and reasoned, Jesus himself drew near, and went with them.
>
> 16 — But their eyes were holden that they should not recognize him.
>
> 17 — And he said unto them, What manner of communications are these that ye have one with another, as ye walk, and are sad?
>
> 18 — And the one of them, whose name was Cleopas, answering said unto him, Art thou only a stranger in Jerusalem, and hast not known the things which are come to pass there in these days?
>
> 19 — And he said unto them, What things? And they said unto him, Concerning Jesus of Nazareth who was a prophet, mighty in deed and word before God and all the people;

20 — And how the chief priests and our rulers delivered him to be condemned to death, and have crucified him.

21 — But we hoped that it had been he who should have redeemed Israel; and, besides all this, TODAY IS THE THIRD DAY SINCE THESE THINGS WERE DONE. (Scofield Bible)

On numerous occasions Jesus told His disciples that He would not only be put to death, but that He would be in the tomb three days and three nights, and would be raised after the third day. The reader will note from the above quoted passage that Cleopas and his companion, while on their way to Emmaus on this very same Sunday, declared TODAY IS THE THIRD DAY since all these things were done. That this conversation took place on the first day of the week is plainly evident from verse 13, for here it is stated that it was THAT SAME DAY on which the women found the tomb empty.

After His resurrection, Jesus was seen by His disciples forty days before His ascension. During this period there are recorded two instances when He met with His disciples in an assembly. The first of these, which occurred on the very day He was raised, is reported in John 20:19, as follows: "Then the SAME DAY at evening, being THE FIRST DAY OF THE WEEK, when the doors were shut where the disciples were assembled for fear of the Jews, came Jesus and stood in the midst, and saith unto them, Peace be unto you."

Like several other verses, this one stands in Armstrong's way. What answer does he have for it? "Let us examine this carefully," he tells his disciples, "for some claim this was a religious service called for the purpose of celebrating the Resurrection. But notice this is the *same* first day of the week that FOLLOWED the Sabbath. It was Jesus' first opportunity to appear to His disciples . . ."[7]

Did this first meeting really occur on the first day of the week *only* because "it was Jesus' first opportunity to appear to His disciples"? Who said so? If He arose on Saturday afternoon, on the Jewish Sabbath, as Armstrong claims, why could He not have appeared to His disciples on the Sabbath? In His resurrected body He was fully able to appear anywhere, instantaneously, just as He appeared and "stood among them," even though the doors were shut.

John also records that Jesus again appeared before His assembled disciples the next Sunday. In the twentieth chapter, verse 26, he writes: "And after eight days again his disciples were within, and Thomas with them: then came Jesus, the doors being shut, and stood in the midst, and said, Peace be unto you."

This particular meeting of His disciples (that is, His church) is ignored by Armstrong, perhaps because of the statement *eight days,* which might at first glance seem to place it on a Monday. But this is not so. Though we reckon from Sunday to Sunday as seven days, the Jews calculated it as "eight days," counting in both Sundays.

Jesus' meeting with His disciples on these first two Sundays was the beginning of a tradition which has continued from that time until our own day. That the church afterward kept this *stated day* as a weekly memorial of the Resurrection is plain from the reading of Acts 20:7, which states: "And upon the FIRST DAY OF THE WEEK, when the disciples CAME TOGETHER to break bread, Paul PREACHED unto them, ready to depart on the morrow; and continued his speech until midnight." This church at Troas, then, met on the "first day of the week," and on that day heard Paul preach. To claim that this was not so would be to charge Luke, its author, with a deliberate misrepresentation of the facts, something no *true* Christian would be inclined to do. More evidence of this tradition can be found in the following directions from Paul to the church at Corinth: "Upon the FIRST DAY OF THE WEEK let every one of you lay by him in store, as God hath prospered him, that there be no gatherings when I come" (I Corinthians 16:2). Thus, the giving of the weekly tithe in Paul's own day was on Sunday, according to apostolic instructions. So it is to this very day.

The Armstrong believers make much to-do over the fact that, according to the Scriptures, the apostles on several occasions entered and taught in the synagogues on the Sabbath Day. They cite this as "proof" that the early *true* Christians "had started keeping the Sabbath Day, and went to church on that day." [8] But what kind of proof is this? On what other day would the apostles—in their mission to convert their fellow Jews—enter into the synagogues to teach? On Monday? The Jews did not assemble at their synagogues on Monday—nor on Tuesday, nor Wednesdays, nor Thursdays, nor Fridays. The Jews' religious assembly was on Saturdays, *their* Sabbath. Therefore, it seems altogether logical and reasonable that the apostles, if they hoped to have an audience, would make their appearances in the synagogues coincide with the day when the Jews would also be gathered there.

It is an indisputable fact that the earliest church writers mentioned Sunday as the day the church was accustomed to meet. On this they were unanimous. "There is," writes historian Philip Schaff, "no dissenting voice." [9]

Probably the earliest of these writings is a short manual of moral instruction, church discipline, and church order known as *The Teaching of the Twelve Apostles,* or as *The Didache.* Held in great repute by the early church, it was in circulation probably as early as 60 A.D.[10] Its instruction to the early Christians concerning the weekly gathering of the church is as follows: "On the Lord's own day* assemble in common to break bread and offer thanks; but first confess your sins, so that your sacrifice may be pure." [11]

Ignatius, who Eusebius says was the successor to Peter in the episcopate of the church at Antioch and who later was thrown to the wild beasts at Rome for his faith, was one of the earliest Christian writers to leave us a record (seven letters) of the traditions established by the primitive church.* In his epistles, Ignatius speaks of Christians as "no longer observing the Sabbath, but living in the observance of the Lord's Day, on which also Our Life rose again."[12] Ignatius died in a Roman arena just after the close of the first century, about 110 A.D. The author of the *Epistle of Barnabas*** about this same time wrote: "We keep the eighth day for rejoicing, in which also Jesus rose from the dead, and having been manifested [to His disciples], ascended into the heavens.***[13] Also within this same time period (112 A.D.), Pliny the Younger, whom Trajan had sent to govern the province of Bithynia in Asia Minor, wrote the Roman emperor that it was the practice of Christians in Bithynia on this "stated day" to assemble before daylight to sing hymns to Christ as a God, and to bind themselves by a *sacramentum* not to do any wicked deed, or never to commit fraud, theft or adultery, or bear false witness. [14]

The church's custom of meeting before daylight on Sundays, as mentioned by Pliny, was necessary in those early days. At that time, Sunday was a common workday, and after this early worship service the Christians were obliged to be about their daily chores, for many were of the poorer class or slaves, in the hire of others. Where a day of rest was observed, it was usually on Saturdays, following the custom of the Jews who continued to keep the Sabbath in the countries to which they had been dispersed. Gradually, however, Sunday took over as the weekly rest day as the Christians advanced in numbers and in social position. [15] It was not until the time of Constantine (321 A.D.), however, that the former workday received official sanction as the Christian day of rest throughout the Roman Empire.

Irenaeus' testimony on the Lord's day is important. This, he says, writing about 170 A.D., was celebrated on the first day of the week. He also writes that the Jewish Sabbath was merely a symbolical and typical ordinance, while noting that Abraham "without observance of Sabbaths believed in God."[16] Irenaeus as a young man sat at the feet of the aged Polycarp, who was a disciple of the Apostle John and bishop of Smyrna. Irenaeus himself has been described as "the most considerable Christian theologian of the 2nd century." [17]

Finally, the testimony of Justin, who is traditionally known as "the Martyr," for the reason that he paid the full price for his faith at Rome about 165 A.D., is worthy of our consideration. In his *Apology to Caesar,* Justin, unmindful of his own safety, boldly sets out to explain to the emperor the beliefs of the Christian Church in an attempt to exonerate fellow Christians from false charges brought against them by persecutors from the ranks of both pagans and Jews. "Henceforward," he wrote, "we constantly remind one another of these things. The rich among us come to the aid of the poor, and we always stay together. For all the favors we enjoy we bless the Creator of all, through His Son Jesus Christ and through the Holy Spirit. On the day which is called Sunday we have a common assembly of all who live in the cities or in the outlying districts, and the memoirs of the Apostles or the writings of the Prophets are read, as long as there is time. Then, when the reader has finished, the president of the assembly verbally admonishes and invites all to imitate such examples of virtue. Then we all stand up together and offer up our prayers, and, as we said before, after we finish our prayers, bread and wine are presented. . .The Eucharistic elements are distributed and consumed by those present, and to those who are absent they are sent through the deacons." [18]

Sunday, Justin told the emperor, was the day honored by Christians "because it is the first day on which God, transforming the darkness and prime matter, created the world; and our Savior Jesus Christ arose from the dead on the same day."[19]

The confusion over the Jewish Sabbath law in regards to Christians began at an early date. As the Apostle Paul and Barnabas went from one city to another preaching the good news, "certain men" from Judea followed their trail, teaching that the Mosaic Law—including circumcision and observance of the Sabbath—must be obeyed by the Christians, whether Jew or Gentile, with the result that the churches established by Paul and Barnabas were thrown into confusion. Disputes between Paul and these Judaizers resulted in the first church council meeting at Jerusalem, the details of which are given in Acts 15.

The decision of this first Christian council was to affirm Paul and Barnabas in their teaching and to issue a declaration to that effect. This letter is recorded in the Holy Scriptures as follows:

> The apostles and elders and brethren send greeting unto the brethren who are of the Gentiles in Antioch and Syria and Cilicia:
> Forasmuch as we have heard that certain who went out from us have troubled you with words, subverting your souls, saying, Ye must be circumcised, and KEEP THE LAW, to whom WE GAVE NO SUCH COMMANDMENT, it seemed good unto us, being assembled WITH ONE ACCORD, to send chosen men unto you with our beloved Barnabas and Paul ... We have sent, therefore, Judas and Silas, who shall also tell you the same things by mouth. For it seemed good to the Holy Spirit, and to us, to lay upon you no greater burden than these necessary things: THAT YE ABSTAIN FROM THINGS OFFERED TO IDOLS, AND FROM BLOOD, AND FROM THINGS STRANGLED, AND FROM FORNICATION; FROM WHICH, IF YE KEEP YOURSELVES, YE SHALL DO WELL. Fare ye well. (Acts 15:23-25, 27-29 Scofield Bible)

This then was the council's answer to the two questions put to them concerning circumcision and the keeping of the Law. They told the Christians in Antioch and Syria and Cilicia that they had given "no such commandment" previously, nor was any such commandment forthcoming now. The only restrictions the council at Jerusalem placed upon these churches were those concerning things which might cause some of the Christian believers from among the Jews to stumble, just as circumcision and the Law would have caused many of the Gentiles to stumble.

The Apostles' letter was received with great joy at Antioch (verses 30, 31). The Jerusalem letter was a major setback for the Judaizers following Paul and Barnabas, but it did not eliminate the problem entirely. Certain ones continued to follow Paul, attempting at every opportunity to subvert or compromise his teachings. One has only to look at his epistles to discern his deep and growing concern that the churches he had established were still being seduced and corrupted by these false brethren in his absence. His anguish is nowhere more evident than in his letter to the Galatians, where he writes: "Ye did run well; who did hinder you that ye should not obey the truth? This persuasion cometh not of him that called you...For, brethren, ye have been called UNTO LIBERTY; only use not liberty for an occasion to the flesh, BUT BY LOVE SERVE ONE ANOTHER" (Galatians 5:7-8,13 Scofield Bible).

Again, to the same congregation, he declared: "Nevertheless then, when ye knew not God, ye did service unto them which by nature are no gods. But now, after ye have known God, or rather are known by God, how turn ye again to the WEAK and BEGGARLY ELEMENTS, unto which ye desire again TO BE IN BONDAGE. Ye OBSERVE DAYS, and months, and times, and years. I AM AFRAID OF YOU, LEST I HAVE BESTOWED UPON YOU LABOR IN VAIN" (Galatians 4:8-11 Scofield Bible).

Writing on this same subject to the Gentiles at Colossae, he again advised: "Let no man, therefore, judge you in food, or in drink, or in respect of a feast day, or of the new moon, OR OF A SABBATH DAY" (Colossians 2:16 Scofield Bible).

It is significant that the efforts of these Judaizers, though the cause of some trouble at first, eventually came to naught. Soon Sunday—though it was still a common workday—was recognized by all as the Christian day of worship. Even such a heretical sect as the Ebionites, who thought that "the observance of the law was altogether necessary," including the Sabbath and "other discipline of the Jews," did not dispute this. "They also," commented Eusebius, "celebrate the Lord's day very much like us, in commemoration of his resurrection." [20]

CHAPTER VIII

THE WEDNESDAY CRUCIFIXION THEORY

Some years ago the *Sunday School Times* published an article in which, by reconciling the Scriptures of all four Gospels, it was established that Christ was actually crucified on a Wednesday, and not on "Good Friday," as Christendom has long believed. The resurrection, according to this revised chronology, occurred on Saturday afternoon.

These findings were given little attention by the Church at the time, but they have proved a boon to Armstrong for the promotion of Sabbath-keeping by Christians. He has used them to convince literally tens of thousands that the resurrection took place on the Sabbath and not on the first day of the week, which is the day celebrated by most other churches.

It is quite true, as the *Sunday School Times* stated, that Christ was crucified on Wednesday. No other conclusion can possibly be reached after studying the Scriptures which are offered as proof. However, the claim that the resurrection was on the Sabbath is entirely false, as we shall see in a moment. But first, for the benefit of those who are unfamiliar with this study, historical evidence for this conclusion should be established.

Looking again to ecclesiastical history, we find that the early churches eventually came to disagree as to the day on which Christ was crucified. Some observed Fridays as "days of penance, or watch-days, and half-fasting (which lasted till three o'clock in the afternoon.)" [1] Other churches observed Wednesdays as the "weekly commemoration of the sufferings and death of the Lord." [2] Friday "seemed" to have the support of Matthew, Mark, Luke, and John. Wednesday was but a tradition, with perhaps the chief argument in its favor being that once the Friday tradition was established it would seem very difficult indeed for the Wednesday date to have gained any acceptance whatever. So, of the two, Wednesday appears, for this reason, to have been the earliest.

The *Didascalia,* an early Christian work which is preserved in Syriac, but which was probably written originally in Greek, supports the Wednesday tradition. In this work the apostles are quoted as saying that it was on Tuesday evening that they ate the Passover with Jesus, and on Wednesday that he was taken captive and held in custody in the house of Caiaphas. [3] Also, Epiphanius, a post-Nicene writer, protests that Jesus could not have been arrested on the night of Thursday-Friday; the false tradition for him is that which puts the Last Supper on Thursday evening; the correct one is that which puts it on Tuesday evening. [4] Moreover, an early chronology worked out by Victorinus of Pettau arrives at the conclusion that Jesus *must* have been arrested on a Wednesday. [5] Finally, there is a certain amount of evidence found in the writings of the Early Church Fathers for the Last Supper having taken place on the 13th of Nisan, i.e., Tuesday evening. [6]

Of course, Friday eventually came to be recognized as the crucifixion day. Gradually, the Wednesday tradition disappeared from the scene altogether, with its memory surviving in only a few of the early writings. The "Good Friday" mistake, which was an honest one, was the result of an erroneous assumption that during the week Jesus was arrested, tried, and put to death there was but one Sabbath. Actually there were two, and clear distinction is made between them in John's Gospel. Moreover, rather than contradicting him, which might seem to be the case, the other three Gospels bear him out.

Although universally accepted now, the Friday crucifixion date has really caused a great deal of distress among Bible scholars and commentators. Their problem has been to reconcile Jesus' statement that He would be three days and three nights in the tomb with the thirty-six hours that can be counted from the time of His burial at sunset Friday until the women found the sepulcher empty at early dawn on Sunday. In their attempts to make the facts agree, Bible scholars have generally explained that Jesus was entombed just before sundown beginning the Jewish Sabbath and these few minutes should count as one whole day; then the Sabbath was another day; then early Sunday morning should be reckoned as another day. But this hardly fits the time period that Jesus Himself gave when He told the Pharisees: "An evil and adulterous generation seeks for a sign; but no sign shall be given to it except the sign of the prophet Jonah. For as Jonah was THREE DAYS AND THREE NIGHTS in the belly of the whale, so will the Son of man be THREE DAYS AND THREE NIGHTS in the heart of the earth" (Matthew 12:39-40 RSV).

French Bible scholar Maurice Goguel has pointed up the perplexity that he and others have faced in attempting a solution. "No interpretation however subtle," he writes, "can harmonize this statement [i.e., the 'sign of the prophet Jonah'] with the idea that Jesus was buried on Friday night and rose again on Sunday morning." [7]

The problem confronting Goguel and other scholars down through the centuries resulted from their misunderstanding about the *two* Sabbaths. Having two *holy convocations* in one week was nothing unusual, however. It was, in fact, a very common occurrence since the Jews were obliged under the Law to observe additional Sabbaths held in conjunction with their several festivals throughout the year. These Sabbaths, called "high days," are proclaimed in Leviticus 23. The Passover, of course, always fell on the 14th of Nisan. This was the day on which the paschal lamb, representative of the sacrifice Christ Himself would make, was slain by each Jewish family. The Feast of Unleavened Bread, commemorating the Hebrews' deliverance from Egypt by God, was observed the next day, on the 15th of Nisan. This was a "high day," sometimes called the "Great Sabbath." Unleavened bread was eaten for seven days, and on the seventh day, or on the 22nd of Nisan, there was yet another Sabbath. Except on occasions when the high Sabbath fell on the same day as the weekly Sabbath (or when they fell upon succeeding days), it was necessary to have two *days of preparation,* one for each Sabbath.

The Apostle John, while describing the events of the crucifixion, took pains to define the difference between these two sabbaths in the following manner: "Since it was the day of Preparation, in order to prevent the bodies from remaining on the cross on the sabbath (for that sabbath was a HIGH DAY), the Jews asked Pilate that their legs might be broken, and that they might be carried away" (John 19:31 RSV).

Keeping in mind that the Jews counted their days as beginning at sundown,* and not at midnight as we calculate time, the actual chronology of the crucifixion week looked something like this:

WEDNESDAY
(14th of Nisan)

—During the early hours of the evening beginning this day, immediately following the Lord's Supper, Jesus was arrested and brought before Caiaphas and the Sanhedrin, where He was questioned during the night hours (Mark 14:55-65).

—When morning came, the chief priests and elders delivered Jesus to Pontius Pilate, hoping to have Him put to death. Jesus appeared before Pilate, then before King Herod, who returned Him to Pilate's jurisdiction, where the chief priests and rulers of the people prevailed upon the governor to crucify the Galilean (Matthew 27:1-2, Luke

23:7, 11, 20-23).

—At the "third hour" (i.e., 9 a.m.), Jesus was nailed to the cross (Mark 15:25).

—Shortly after the "ninth hour" (3 p.m.), Jesus cried out and gave up the ghost (Luke 23:44-46).

—When evening was come,* Joseph of Arimathea went to Pilate and asked for the body. He and Nicodemus, having taken the body down from the cross, placed Jesus in His tomb. This was accomplished at sundown. We know this from Luke's account of the burial. The exact time is given in the following statement: "It was the day of Preparation [Wednesday], and the sabbath [Thursday] was beginning" (Luke 23:54 RVS). It was at this time that the women who had come with Him from Galilee, who had sat opposite the sepulcher while the burial was in progress (Mat. 27:61 RSV), saw the tomb and how the body was laid (Luke 23:55, Mark 15:47), and then returned home to prepare spices and ointments (Luke 23:56), but this work was not done until the following day since it was *now* the high Sabbath.

THURSDAY
(15th of Nisan)

The only activity we have recorded on this high Sabbath is that of the chief priests and the Pharisees appearing before Pilate to ask that the tomb be made secure "until the third day, lest his disciples go and steal him away, and tell the people, 'He has risen from the dead' " (Matthew 27:64 RSV).

FRIDAY
(16th of Nisan)

The feast-day Sabbath over, Mary Magdalene, and Mary, the mother of James, and Salome BOUGHT spices (which could not have been purchased until the Sabbath was ended), and returned home to prepare them with ointments (Mark 16:1).

SATURDAY
(17th of Nisan)

The weekly Sabbath. The spices having been purchased and prepared the previous day, Mary Magdalene and the other women *again* "rested ... according to the commandment" (Luke 23:56).

SUNDAY
(18th of Nisan)

At early dawn, Mary Magdalene, Joanna, and Mary, the mother of James, "and certain others," went to the tomb, taking the spices which they had prepared with them, and found the stone rolled away, and the tomb empty (Luke 24:1-3).

The resurrection, Armstrong claims, took place on the afternoon of the weekly Sabbath. This, at first glance, might seem correct. The Lord died on the cross just after 3 p.m. on that Wednesday. But the "sign of the prophet Jonah" was to be counted from the time of His entombment, which was, according to Luke, at sunset, marking the beginning of the day Thursday. The next sunset, ushering in Friday, would count as one day. The next sunset, beginning the weekly Sabbath day, would mark the second day. At sundown on this day Christ arose from the dead, at the end of the third full day. But *this* sundown was the official beginning of *the first day of the week.* This is the day upon which the Scriptures say Christ was resurrected, and which has been commemorated by the Christian Church ever since.*

(For a further clarification of the Wednesday crucifixion theory, see Appendix I.)

CHAPTER IX

ARMSTRONG AND THE EUCHARIST

Since the Armstrong flock is somewhat widely scattered, and since they have only "167 local churches" to serve their far-flung, worldwide congregation of 50,000 baptized members, the question of how they observe the Lord's Supper presents itself.[1] Since they frequently claim that they are the only *true* church, their faithfulness in following this command by Jesus may be particularly revealing, for certainly the *true* church should be found obedient in the *correct* keeping of this most important ordinance.

In the time of the apostles, the Lord's Supper or Eucharist was observed whenever Christians gathered for their church meetings. Giving instructions for this, the Apostle Paul wrote the following to the church at Corinth: "I passed on to you what I received from the Lord himself, namely, that on the night he was betrayed the Lord Jesus took a loaf, and after thanking God he broke it, saying, 'This means my body broken for you; do this in memory of me.' In the same way he took the cup after supper, saying, 'This cup means the new covenant ratified by my blood; as often as you drink it, do it in memory of me.' For as often as you eat this loaf and drink this cup, you proclaim the Lord's death until he comes" (I Corinthians 11:23-26 Moffatt).

According to Armstrong, the sacrament of the Lord's Supper, as described here by Paul, should be observed only once a year. His death, he says, should be proclaimed only on the Passover.

This is quite a departure from the tradition of both the protestant church, which holds communion services either weekly or monthly or at least quarterly, depending upon the denomination, and the early church, which partook of the consecrated elements as often as they met, according to apostolic precedent.[2]

Yet Armstrong maintains that his way was the one actually followed by the early *true* church, the rest being deceived. "The disciples," he declares, "continued to observe Passover annually, now in the form of the Lord's Supper."[3]

For a fact, the disciples of the early church did observe the Passover, which was, and still is, the oldest and most important annual festival of the church. Somewhere along the way, however, it picked up the name Easter. But the second part of Armstrong's statement—that the Passover was now "in the form" of the Lord's Supper—has no foundation in fact, whatsoever.

As proof for this we have a number of instances recorded in the New Testament where the church is shown gathering to break bread on days other than the Passover. One of these, for example, followed Paul's journey to Troas to preach. Luke, the author of Acts, writes that the Apostle and his party "sailed away from Philippi after the days of unleavened bread, and came unto them to Troas in five days; where we abode seven days" (Acts 20:6). Now the *days of unleavened bread,* as we have already seen, is the Jewish festival immediately following the Passover on the 14th of Nisan. The Passover, then, had been observed almost two weeks prior to their coming ashore at Troas on the 27th of Nisan. Yet Luke, on this occasion, reports: "And upon the first day of the week, when the disciples came together *to break bread,* Paul preached unto them, ready to depart on the morrow ..." (Acts 20:7). There can be no doubt that this was a church meeting, for those that came together are called disciples, and it is further stated that "Paul *preached* unto them." The breaking of the bread was the Eucharist. How does Armstrong contend with this?

"The truth is," he explains, "NOWHERE IN THE BIBLE is the expression 'breaking of bread,' or 'to break bread,' used to signify observance of the Lord's Supper." All these instances, he adds, "referred only to eating food as a meal, not to a Communion service."[4]

This is, of course, contrary to what we have been told elsewhere by Paul. That the Eucharist was observed most frequently is plainly seen in his letter to the Corinthians, in which he admonishes those of *this* church for improper conduct in celebrating the Lord's Supper. "First of all," he writes, "in your church meetings I am told that cliques prevail. And I partly believe it; there must be parties among you, if genuine Christians are to be recognized. But this makes it impossible for you TO EAT THE 'LORD'S' SUPPER when you hold YOUR GATHERINGS" (I Corinthians 11:18-20 Moffatt).

In view of what Paul has said here it would seem difficult indeed to pretend these were common meals. In fact, the Apostle himself, later in the same chapter, further distinguishes between the two, as he gave these additional instructions: "Well then, my brothers, when you gather for a meal, wait for one another; and IF ANYONE IS HUNGRY, let him eat AT HOME. You must not gather, only to incur condemnation" (I Corinthians 11:33-34 Moffatt).

Clearly then, some of the Corinthians had begun to use the table at these "church-meetings" improperly, turning this feast held in thankful remembrance of His atoning death into common meals. Common meals to satisfy hunger, Paul said, should be eaten AT HOME.

It should be noted, too, in passing, that it was possible to incur the Lord's condemnation at these meals. This would not be the case if they were only common.

Actually, Armstrong's error concerning the Eucharist results from a basic misunderstanding. In the days of the apostles, the Eucharist and the Agape were jointly celebrated. On these frequent occasions the bread, representing Christ's body, was broken, and the wine, representative of the blood He shed for the New Covenant, was distributed. This is the reason Paul admonishes the Corinthians to "wait for one another" so that this most solemn

- 62 -

church ordinance could be observed properly. The Agape, or "love-feast," followed the communion service. Concerning these, Philip Schaff has written: "In the apostolic period the eucharist was celebrated daily in connection with a simple meal of brotherly love *(agape),* in which the Christians, in communion with their common Redeemer, forgot all distinctions of rank, wealth, and culture, and felt themselves to be members of one family of God. But this childlike exhibition of brotherly unity became more and more difficult as the church increased, and led to all sorts of abuses, such as we find rebuked in th. Corinthians by Paul. The love-feasts, therefore, which indeed were no more enjoined by law than the community of goods at Jerusalem, were gradually severed from the eucharist, and in the course of the second and third centuries gradually disappeared."[5]

In addition to Paul, Ignatius, whom we have mentioned previously, gives us a good idea of the early church's custom in observing the Lord's Supper. Writing the following in a letter while on his way to Rome, bound in chains, he made this appeal to the Christians at Ephesus: "Make an effort, then, to come more frequently to celebrate God's Eucharist and to offer praise. For when you meet frequently in the same place, the forces of Satan are overthrown, and his baneful influence is neutralized by the unanimity of your faith. Peace is a precious thing: it puts an end to every war waged by heavenly or earthly enemies."[6]

For a final word on this we return to Justin Martyr's *Apology to Caesar,* from which we have already quoted: "On the day which is called Sunday we have a common assembly of all who live in the cities or in the outlying districts, and the memoirs of the Apostles or the writings of the Prophets are read, as long as there is time ... After we finish our prayers, bread and wine are presented ... The Eucharistic elements are distributed and consumed by those present, and to those who are absent they are sent through the deacons."[7]

CHAPTER X

THE TRINITY DENIED

There is no Trinity, the Armstrong cult claims. Like Jehovah's Witnesses, they believe there are only two Persons in the Godhead—the Father and the Son. The Holy Spirit, they say, is only a "force." They even go further than that. All who believe in the Trinity of the Godhead are pagans and heretics, they declare.

This view was expressed by Dr. C.P. Meredith in an article in *The Plain Truth* in 1960. He wrote: "Note now that the pagans termed the Holy Spirit a 'Being' such as the Father and Son. They wrongly made a Trinity. Satan was confusing mankind." [1]

In 1962, Armstrong himself proclaimed: "'The theologians' and 'higher critics' have blindly accepted the heretical and false doctrine (introduced by pagan false prophets who crept in) that the Holy Spirit is a Third Person ... This," he says, "limits God to three persons." [2]

But the Holy Spirit is many times referred to in the Bible by the personal pronoun "he" or "him." What about this? And what of the numerous occasions when Jesus Himself spoke of the Holy Spirit as a Person, as, for example, in this passage from John 16:7-14 (Moffatt translation):

"Yet—I am telling you the truth—my going is for your good. If I do not depart, the Helper will not come to you; whereas, if I go, I will send *him* to you. And when *he* comes, *he* will convict the world, convincing men of sin, of righteousness, and of judgment: of sin, because they do not believe in me; of righteousness, because I go to the Father and you see me no more; of judgment, because the Prince of this world has been judged. I have still much to tell you, but you cannot bear it at present. However, when the Spirit of truth comes, *he* will lead you into all the truth; for *he* will not speak of *his* own accord, *he* will say whatever *he* is told, and *he* will disclose to you what is to come. *He* will glorify me for *he* will draw upon what is mine and disclose it to you. All that the Father has is mine; that is why I say, '*he* will draw upon what is mine and disclose it to you.' "

How do the architects of the Armstrong religion explain this? The explanation, they say, is very simple. In the Greek, as in the French, many words are given a masculine or feminine gender. The Greek pronouns used to designate the Paraclete or Holy Spirit are in the neuter gender, and thus should be translated "it." Unfortunately, in the King James Version of the New Testament, there are a couple of instances* when the Spirit is referred to by the impersonal pronouns "it" and "itself." These are in error, and the King James translators are found to be inconsistent *even* with themselves in the numerous places that they have used the personal pronouns "he," "him," and "himself," in referring to the Holy Spirit. These mistranslations, incidentally, are also invariably peculiar to the King James Version, with almost all other translations using the personal pronouns. There is, however, no real need here to go into lengthy or detailed debate over the accuracy of various translations. That the Spirit is indeed a "Person" or "Being" can be proved conclusively from the Holy Scriptures, as we shall see from the following passage from the Acts of the Apostles:

"Now in Caesarea there was a man called Cornelius, a captain in the Italian regiment, a religious man, who reverenced God with all his household, who was liberal in his alms to the People, and who constantly prayed to God. About three o'clock in the afternoon HE DISTINCTLY SAW in a vision AN ANGEL OF GOD entering and saying to him, 'Cornelius.' He STARED at the ANGEL in terror, saying, 'What is it?' He replied, 'Your prayers and your alms have risen before God as a sacrifice to be remembered. You must now SEND SOME MEN to Joppa for a certain Simon who is surnamed Peter; he is staying with Simon a tanner, whose house stands by the sea' " (Acts 10:1-6 Moffatt).

The reader will recall that this is the same chapter in which Peter's vision of a great sheet being lowered from heaven is recorded. This was God's revelation to him and to the other church leaders that Gentiles should be accepted into the faith *as* Gentiles, and not as Jewish proselytes, requiring circumcision and the keeping of the Law of Moses (see Acts 10:34-35,44-48; 11:1-18). Immediately after this vision, we pick up the narrative at verse 17:

"Peter was quite at a loss to know the meaning of the vision he had seen; but just then the messengers of Cornelius, who had made inquiries for the house of Simon, stood at the door and called out to ask if Simon, surnamed Peter, was staying there. So THE SPIRIT said to Peter, who was pondering over the vision, 'There are three men looking for you! Come, get up and go down, and have no hesitation about accompanying them, FOR IT IS I WHO HAVE SENT THEM' " (Acts 10:17-20 Moffatt).

The reader has already seen at the beginning of this passage that AN ANGEL of God, who is a *being,* appeared to Cornelius and directed him "to send some men to Joppa" for Peter. And in the concluding verses quoted here we are told that the SPIRIT advised Peter to accompany these three men, "for," the Spirit said, "IT IS I WHO HAVE SENT THEM."

It can only be concluded from this, then, that the angel who told Cornelius to *send men,* and the Spirit, who told Peter that He *had sent them* are One and the same Person or Being.

The doctrine of the Holy Spirit as a Person was early accepted by those of the apostolic age. It was, in fact, basic to the Gospel of Christ. According to the teachings of the apostles, the triune God was our Maker, Redeemer, and Sanctifier. This was clearly Paul's idea when he pronounced this benediction at the close of his second epistle to the Corinthians: "The grace of the Lord Jesus Christ, and the love of God, and the communion of the Holy Spirit be with you all" (II Corinthians 13:14 Scofield Bible).

Nor was this giving the Holy Spirit a place alongside God the Father and Jesus Christ the Son an innovation with Paul. For this he had the highest Authority. Christ Himself set forth this revelation of the Trinity in Matthew 28:19 (Socfield Bible), in these words to His disciples: "Go ye, therefore, and teach all nations, baptizing them in the NAME of the Father, and of the Son, and of the Holy Spirit." Also of the Trinity the Apostle John wrote: "For there are THREE that bear record in heaven, the FATHER, the WORD, and the HOLY SPIRIT; and these THREE ARE ONE" (I John 5:7 Scofield Bible).

The mystery of God has not been fully revealed, nor will it be until "the trumpet call to be sounded by the seventh angel" (Rev. 10:7 RSV). We, with our finite minds, cannot begin to comprehend Him. A glimpse into this mystery, however, can be seen in the following verses: "God has revealed to us through the Spirit. For the Spirit searches everything, even the depths of God. For what person knows a man's thoughts except the spirit of the man which is in him" (I Corinthians 2:10-11 RSV). Much can be learned from studying these two verses, but for our purpose the point to be made here is that the Holy Spirit *comprehends.* This naturally presupposes that He has an intelligence to comprehend. Also in I Corinthians 12:11, He is shown to have a will. Paul, writing about the spiritual gifts bestowed upon Christians, explains: "All these are inspired by one and the same SPIRIT, who apportions to each one individually AS HE WILLS" (I Cor. 12:11 RSV). From the account cited from Acts, where He appears to Cornelius as an "Angel of God," He is shown to have not only mobility, but He both hears and speaks. He also has feeling (Ep. 4:30). Moreover, in Mark 3:28-29, Christ Himself warns against blaspheming against the Holy Spirit. The Holy Spirit, then, has the ability to comprehend, He has a will, He moves about, He speaks, He hears, He has feeling, He can be blasphemed.

Until the middle of the fourth century, the doctrine of the Holy Spirit "was never a subject of special controversy." [3] "Antitrinitarism" was confined solely to the ranks of the heretics. [4] Without exception, the ante-Nicene fathers agreed in the two fundamental points, that the Holy Spirit—the sole agent in the application of redemption—is a supernatural divine Being, and that He is an independent Person. [5]

In addition to the Scriptures, we find the Trinity doctrine outlined in ecclesiastical writings as early as Polycarp's time. In his final prayer as he was about to be burned at the stake, Polycarp concluded his petition to God with the following words: ". . .May I be accepted among them in Thy sight today as a rich and pleasing sacrifice. . .And therefore I praise Thee for everything. I bless Thee; I glorify Thee through the eternal and heavenly High Priest Jesus Christ, Thy beloved Son, through whom be glory to Thee TOGETHER with Him and the Holy Spirit, both now and for the ages yet to come. Amen." [6] Also in his *Apology to Caesar*, Justin Martyr explains to the emperor that Christians worship the Creator Father, the Son, and the Holy Spirit. [7] And another ante-Nicene writer, Irenaeus, (170 A.D.), records for us a creed containing twelve articles of the Christian faith which were in use by the early church. Similar to the Apostle's Creed of the post-Nicene era, it contains the following confession:

"We believe

1. . . .in one God the father Almighty, who made heaven and earth, and the sea, and all that in them is;

2. And in one Christ Jesus, the Son of God . . .

3. And in the Holy Ghost . . ."[8]

In concluding this chapter, it is worth noting that if the Holy Spirit is indeed more than the mere "force" that Armstrong calls Him, if He is truly a Third Person in the Trinity, which the Scriptures plainly declare, then it follows that Armstrong is not really acquainted with the Holy Spirit, whom Christ sent to lead the *true* church until the end of this present age.

CHAPTER XI

ARMSTRONG ON JUSTIFICATION AND GRACE

Since they willingly place themselves under the Law, or "within the Law," as they prefer to describe it, what role do they assign such important New Covenant doctrines as *Justification* and *Grace?*

Simply stated, *justification* means that the believing sinner is treated as righteous because Christ, "who knew no sin," bore His sins on the cross, being made "sin for us...that we might be made the righteousness of God IN HIM" (II Cor. 5:21). The accepted orthodox teaching of *grace,* meanwhile, is that Christ imparts HIS RIGHTEOUS-NESS to believers (Rom. 3:21-24), who therefore are "justified by his grace," and who then become "heirs according to the hope of eternal life" (Titus 3:7).

Since both these stand in contrast to the Law (Romans 11:6), which demands righteousness from men by works, how can these be made to fit into a system which still regards the Law of Moses as its guide to salvation?

The orthodox understanding of these doctrines, they simply claim, has been distorted by false ministers from the earliest times, who are guilty of "turning grace into license." As interpreted by the Armstrong cult, both these doctrines are given a substantially different meaning.

"To many people," they say, "JUSTIFICATION means vaguely the same thing 'grace' has meant to so many thousands of deceived persons. It means, to many deceived ones, a 'condition' PERMANENTLY attributed to a Christian. Many people think once a person is 'justified' he is 'MADE RIGHT' from then on! But this is simply untrue.. .Justification is not a *permanent* 'condition' of a Christian. It has to do with the removal and the forgiveness of *past guilt.* . . [Justification] is the *immediate condition* at the exact TIME of his total repentance and surrender to God." [1]

Their *doctrine on grace* is very similar. "Christ DIED in order to ERASE OUR PAST SINS! (Rom. 5:8). THAT IS WHAT GRACE IS! It is the unlimited *mercy* of our God—the unearned, unmerited PARDON of our God, when we totally *repent* of our past sins! ...Grace, then, is God's loving willingness to forgive us of our past *sins!*" [2]

Though these beliefs, at first glance, may seem innocuous, they are quite at variance with traditional church doctrine. The reader should take notice that the emphasis is entirely on "the forgiveness of past guilt" at the "exact TIME" of conversion.

On this point, the elder Armstrong is most emphatic. "We are," he declares, "justified only of SINS THAT ARE PAST. We have remission only of SINS THAT ARE PAST. . ." [3] That's pretty plain talk. It would be hard to misunderstand it. According to this Armstrong doctrine, there can be no justification for any sins or further remission of sins after that one moment when all the sins of the past life of an individual are forgiven at his conversion. What then of Peter? If their teaching on grace and justification be accepted, then this Apostle, who first confessed Christ and subsequently denied Him, would have no more forgiveness. Yet the Scriptures clearly show that Peter was forgiven *again.* However, even in the face of this, Armstrong is still able to maintain that we are justified and have remission only for SINS THAT ARE PAST at the very moment of conversion. From this point on, the Armstrong disciples are taught that they must strictly keep "the Law," that is, the Ten Commandments, and upon this and this alone rests their hope of final salvation.

But do they really believe they can live a perfect enough

life to meet all the requirements that the Law demands? They do. They believe that, with God's help, they can "live, from here on, *righteously, happily.*" [4]

Their official position on this is not left to the second echelon to explain. Herbert Armstrong himself, with the admonition to his critics to "GET THAT STRAIGHT" once and for all on what he teaches, states this part of his gospel in the following words:

"WHY do some religious people today teach that it is all right for Christians to go right on breaking the Law? WHY do they say that GRACE means LICENSE to DISOBEY God's Law? No wonder God found it necessary, through Jude, to warn us to contend earnestly for the FAITH ONCE DELIVERED to the saints by Jesus Christ—for, as you'll read in Jude 3-4, there are certain men crept in unawares—deceiving people—TURNING GRACE INTO LICENSE! They are the ones who accuse us of teaching 'salvation by works.'

"Would a governor PARDON a man convicted of murder so he could continue murdering more and more people? God's merciful PARDON—His GRACE—is bestowed on us *because* we have repented, with a sincere desire to *turn from our wicked ways* of lawlessness. If we are willing to live, from here on, *righteously, happily,* as we should have from the beginning, the merciful and loving God has been willing to GIVE His Son Jesus Christ, who, in turn, was willing to give His LIFE, to square up our PAST law-breaking—to wipe the slate clean, and give us, BY HIS MERCIFUL GRACE, a fresh, clean start.

"So, from here on, *we must* OBEY—unto RIGHTEOUSNESS! (Rom. 6:16).

"Yet *you cannot,* of your own strength, keep the spiritual Law spiritually.

"Now let's really understand *that!*

"Many religious people—many ordained ministers—will tell you, 'It is *impossible* to keep the Law.' Are they telling the truth? What does your Bible say?

"NOTICE! Of the parents of John the Baptist, you will read: 'And they were both righteous before God, *walking in all the commandments* and ordinances of the Lord blameless' (Luke 1:6).

"WHY, if it is *impossible,* did Christ command that IF we would enter into *life,* 'KEEP THE COMMANDMENTS'? (Mat. 19:17.) Of those who claim to 'know the Lord,' often using such sentimental religious phrases as 'Oh, how GOOD it is to know the Lord,' but who teach we should not keep the Commandments, YOUR Bible says this: 'He that saith, "I know Him," and keepeth not His commandments, is a LIAR, and the truth is not in him' (1 John 2:4).

"Yet you cannot, alone of yourself, keep the Law *spiritually!* That is not a contradiction. You can keep the literal letter, but not the spirit. Let's make that plain. . .

"But this SPIRITUAL LAW can be fulfilled—performed—spiritually kept and obeyed—ONLY BY *SPIRITUAL LOVE!* You were not born with that kind of love. You do not have, naturally, the kind of love required to truly keep this great Spiritual Law!

"You must go to God to obtain *that* kind of love. That is a love He gives you through the *living* Christ. That is HIS OWN LOVE. It emanates directly from HIM.

"Now UNDERSTAND! True righteousness is keeping 'ALL THY COMMANDMENTS' (Psalm 119:172). It is performing God's Spiritual Law with the SPIRITUAL LOVE which only God can supply. . .

"So—the VERY SPIRIT by which God imparts to you HIS LIFE—His SALVATION—is also His own LOVE which imparts to you HIS RIGHTEOUSNESS! It is no longer just YOU, in your own power and strength 'keeping the commandments'—it is, spiritually speaking, the living Christ IN you, keeping His Father's Commandments—even as He kept them by this same divine love while He was human here on earth!

"Can you brag, or boast, then, about your righteousness? No—IT IS NOT YOUR RIGHTEOUSNESS—IT IS GOD'S! If Christ, by His GRACE, erased your guilty past, gave you access to God, and now pours forth into and through you the spiritual love that keeps the Law, this is not *your* righteousness, but God's.

"And this is not YOUR 'WORKS'! It is *nothing you earn!*

"God does not 'kid Himself.' Some religious teachers tell you Christ lived a righteous life FOR you 1930 years ago, and since you *'can't* keep the Law,' as they claim, God 'IMPUTES' Christ's righteousness of 19 centuries ago to you—by sort of 'kidding Himself' that you are righteous, while you are given license to still be a spiritual CRIMINAL breaking His Law! God does not impute to you something you do not have.

"Far from this—the *living* Christ by His power *makes* us righteous! He imparts to us power to actually BECOME RIGHTEOUS. It is His DOING." [5]

The key phrase in this rather long explanation is found in the next to the last sentence. They actually believe they "BECOME RIGHTEOUS." They give credit to Christ, but the point is that they actually, in public, in writing, boldly proclaim that they have "BECOME RIGHTEOUS."

This is consistent with their position of regarding themselves as "within the Law," while those who sin—which presumably would include all who are not Armstrong disciples—are said to be "under the Law." It is evident from this that Armstrong and his followers place a lot of confidence in the flesh. This is diametrically opposed to the traditional teaching of the church. The orthodox Christian, though he does his *very* best to do God's will, still believes that he must still rely entirely on God's grace. Let us look at the parable that Christ told in Luke 18:

> 9 – And He [Jesus] spake this parable unto certain which trusted in themselves that they were righteous,

and despised others:

10 — Two men went up into the temple to pray; the one a Pharisee, and the other a publican.

11 — The Pharisee stood and prayed thus with himself, God, I thank thee, that I am not as other men are, extortioners, unjust, adulterers, or even as this publican.

12 — I fast twice in the week, I give tithes of all that I possess.

13 — And the publican, standing afar off, would not lift up so much as his eyes unto heaven, but smote upon his breast, saying, God be merciful to me a sinner.

14 — I tell you, this man went down to his house justified rather than the other: for every one that exalteth himself shall be abased; and he that humbleth himself shall be exalted.

From this account we know that the publican, crying out for mercy, was, in deep distress over his sins. He was sincerely repentant, not even daring to look heavenward, "but smote upon his breast." The picture we have is of a man who had no illusions about himself. On the other hand, we gather that the Pharisee had apparently done *no* harm to others and had attended to *all* the ordinances of God. Having reached such a plateau, he recognized himself as BEING RIGHTEOUS. But God did not recognize him as righteous at all.

In outlining his belief that he and his disciples have been able, in the flesh, to BECOME RIGHTEOUS, Armstrong offers proof texts to show that this is both possible and actually taught by the Bible. He quotes from the Apostle John the following statement: "He that saith, I know him, and keepeth not his commandments, is a liar, and the truth is not in him" (I John 2:4). By *this,* did John mean that we would be able to obey without transgression? Apparently not, for in the very *same* letter, the very *same* John also declared: "If we say that we have no sin, we DECEIVE ourselves, and THE TRUTH IS NOT IN US. If we

CONFESS OUR SINS, he is faithful and just to forgive us our sins, and to cleanse us from all unrighteousness" (I John 1:8-9). Again, in the *same* letter, he wrote: "Sin is the transgression of the law" (I John 3:4). It can safely be concluded from this, then, that the Apostle John fully recognized that even though we should strive with all our heart, soul, and mind to keep Christ's commandments that we, in our frailty, would still commit sins, which would be forgiven us upon confession and sincere repentance.

Now concerning the example Armstrong used of the parents of John the Baptist, it is true, as the Bible states, that they were upright and holy, or as the Greek text puts it, "they were both just in the sight of God," which is the translation of Moffatt and some others. This, however, does not mean they were without sin, for the Bible teaches that Jesus was the only One able to keep the Law perfectly. As for the rest of us, "all have sinned, and come short of the glory of God..." (Romans 3:23). Moreover, "all our righteousnesses," even the very best we are able to do in this flesh, said the prophet Isaiah, "are as filthy rags" before a God so Holy that He cannot bear the sight of sin (Isaiah 64:6).

Armstrong's error here is his illusion that the righteousness required by God is attainable by a legal code. Paul, as a devout Jew, "sought righteousness by works of the law, honestly and earnestly, but in vain; as a Christian he found it, as a free gift of grace, by faith in Christ."[6] Paul's theory of justification, as found in his teaching, shows that Christ actually requires from His disciples "a far better righteousness than the legal righteousness of the Scribes and Pharisees, as a condition of entering the kingdom of heaven, namely, the righteousness of God." [7]

BECAUSE QUESTIANS DO ABUSE THE GRACE OF GOD, SOME EVEN TEACHING A DOCTRINE OF GRACE THAT ABUSES GRACE, ARMSTRONGISM NAS A MEARING — MEN REALLY DO DESIRE IN THEIR HEART FOR RIGHTEOUSNESS OF GOD

CHAPTER XII

ON SALVATION

For the record, the Armstrong sect believes that no one is "saved" in this present age. Neither is one "born again," not even when he becomes a true convert to the Christian faith, according to their teaching. Both these conditions, they say, will not take place until the last day, until the resurrection of the *just*. On both these accounts they are found again in sharp disagreement with the evangelical church.

To 'uphold' his position on this, Armstrong likes to point to Romans 5:8-10, which states: "But God commendeth his love toward us in that, while we were yet sinners, Christ died for us. Much more then, being now justified by his blood, we shall be saved from wrath through Him. For if, when we were enemies, we were reconciled to God by the death of his Son, much more, being reconciled, we SHALL BE SAVED by His life" (Scofield Bible).

"LOOK AT IT!" he tells us. "It says 'we SHALL BE saved.' *Not* that we already are saved. It says 'being now justified' but it does NOT say 'being now SAVED.' It says 'we SHALL BE'—yes, in the FUTURE—saved. That is still FUTURE! SEE IT with your own eyes. Don't believe ME. Don't believe preachers who say you are already, now, saved! JUST BELIEVE THESE PLAIN WORDS IN YOUR Bible!

"It IS," he then declares, "real plain, isn't it?" [1]

No, it isn't.

Why? What's wrong with it?

The error here is that what is being taught is only partly

true. Many other Scriptures which clearly show salvation as a process have been excluded and ignored. As an illustration (and also for correction) a few of these are listed below:

> And He [Jesus] said to the woman, "Your faith HAS SAVED YOU; go in peace." (Luke 7:50 RSV)

> And Jesus said to him, "TODAY salvation HAS COME to this house. . ." (Luke 19:9 RSV)

> For in this hope we WERE SAVED. (Romans 8:24 RSV)

> Besides this you know what hour it is, how it is full time now for you to wake from sleep. For SALVATION IS NEARER to us now than when we first believed. (Romans 13:11 RSV)

> For the word of the cross is folly to those who are perishing, but to us who ARE BEING SAVED it is the power of God. (I Corinthians 1:18 RSV)

> For by grace you HAVE BEEN SAVED through faith. (Ephesians 2:8 RSV)

These, along with the Romans passage used by Armstrong, are sufficient to show that God has given us complete assurance of our salvation from the moment of our conversion, and that this assurance continues with us, unfailing, in the present, and that it is promised us in the age yet to come. We do not, in other words, have to wait fearfully, not ever being quite sure of our redemption.

"Too many who have been saved," says Herbert Lockyer—a name which should be familiar to most Bible students—"are ignorant of the fact that their salvation covers the journey between their conversion and death or the return of Christ. Because He continues His ministry in glory, Christ's salvation is unfailing (Hebrews 7:24, 25)."[2]

"Salvation," according to *The New Scofield Reference Bible,* "is in three tenses: (1) The Christian *has been* saved from the guilt and penalty of sin. (2) The Christian *is being* saved from the habit and dominion of sin. And (3) the Christian *will be* saved at the Lord's return, from all the bodily infirmities that are the result of sin and God's curse upon the sinful world, and brought into entire conformity to Christ."

It would be unfair not to mention that Armstrong has, in

other writings, modified his position on *salvation.* In 1967, in his booklet, *What Do You Mean... "The Unpardonable Sin"?* he acknowledges these other Scriptures, then explains to his disciples: "Actually, the Bible speaks of salvation in *three* ways—or as a process in *three* stages if we wish to become theologically technical." [3]

Needless to say, too many false doctrines have been spread about, all because their authors have failed to be *theologically technical.*

We come now to a most intriguing feature of the Armstrong salvation plan. As noted in a previous chapter, a "Millennium Kingdom," according to the teaching of Christ, the prophets, and the apostles, will follow this present age. This thousand-year reign by Christ and His saints on this earth is the subject of numerous Scriptures, and is set forth in a most definite statement in Revelation 20:2, 4, 7. This was a basic doctrine of the early church. Such early church writers as Barnabas, Papias, Irenaeus, Justin, Julius Africanus, Lactantius, and others, have left us a clear record on this. The Armstrong school is in agreement with the millennial view, but even here they have added some new and interesting wrinkles.

The Bible tells of two resurrections. In their studies of the Scriptures, however, the Armstrong cult sees three. It has also been accepted from the times of the primitive church that the rule of Christ and His saints will last for a thousand years, until He has put all His enemies under His feet (I Cor. 15:25), and *then* the kingdom is to be delivered to God the Father (I Cor. 15:24). In the Armstrong scheme of things, however, it has been necessary to add another hundred-year reign at the close of the millennium to fit in with their eschatological timetable. For want of a better name this period might best be described as a "mini-millennium." As scriptural authority for this teaching, Armstrong and his ministers point to Isaiah 65:20. Here in this chapter, while giving us a glimpse of the kingdom to come, the prophet Isaiah declares: "There shall be no more thence an infant of days, nor an old man that hath not filled his days: for the child shall die an hundred years old; but the sinner being an hundred years old shall be accursed."

This period, however, will be preceded by the first two resurrections. The first of these is the "resurrection of the just," which will be at Christ's second coming (Luke 14:14, Rev. 20:4). The second resurrection, and the final one according to orthodox teaching, is that of "THE REST of the dead" mentioned in Revelation 20:5 (RSV), who "did not come to life until the thousand years were ended."

It is at this point that, according to Armstrong, the "mini-millennium" will begin, and at the end of this one hundred years will follow the "third resurrection," which will be of all the "evil dead."

This "mini-millennium" and the "third resurrection" preached in the Armstrong gospel can be found, they say, in the twentieth chapter of Revelation. This account reads:

> 5 — But the rest of the dead lived not again until the thousand years were finished. . .
>
> 11 — And I saw a great white throne, and him that sat on it, from whose face the earth and the heaven fled away, and there was found no place for them.
>
> 12 — And I saw the dead, small and great, stand before God, and the books were opened; and another book was opened, which is the book of life. And the dead were judged out of those things which were written in the books, according to their works.
>
> 13 — And the sea gave up the dead that were in it, and death and hades delivered up the dead that were in them; and they were judged every man according to their works.
>
> 14 — And death and hades were cast into the lake of fire. This is the second death.
>
> 15 — And whosoever was not found written in the book of life was cast into the lake of fire. (Scofield Bible)

They say the "rest of the dead" in verse 5 are all those who have been born since Adam who "NEVER HAD A PREVIOUS CHANCE" for salvation. With the millennium over, these people, who were "spiritually blinded," will now—according to Armstrong—be given their first opportunity for salvation during the one hundred years to follow. [4] Giving a further explanation of this particular feature of the Armstrong gospel, Dr. C.P. Meredith, a fellow worker with Armstrong, writes: "Even the WORST *of the sinners who never had a chance will be in this* RESURRECTION for even the inhabitants of SODOM will be there!" [5]

This "mini-millennium" occurs after verse 12. Verse 13, they teach, reveals the "third resurrection." These in this resurrection, explains Dr. Meredith, "are the evil dead. . . who deliberately decided they did not want to be ruled by God. . .These are they who, after being begotten by God, rebelled, and those who have lived contrary to God's way of life and have refused to repent, be baptized, and thus receive the gift of the Holy Spirit. These are cast into the lake of fire which is described in verse 14 as the Second Death. It is an everlasting death!" [6]

Meredith admits that, at first glance, "it seems strange that there are so many resurrections." But this, he explains, is because "God is going to enlarge his KINGDOM gradually. An increasing number will be given immortality at each resurrection." [7]

This is difficult to understand. In the first place, it doesn't sound plausible that the sole purpose for three resurrections is because God merely wants to "enlarge his KINGDOM gradually." Too, Meredith states that this enlargement is to be accomplished with "each" resurrection, that is, all three resurrections. Yet, he himself declares elsewhere in the same article that the third resurrection are "the evil dead" who are to be "cast into the lake of fire." If this be so, it follows that the kingdom will not be enlarged from among these who, he adds, "deliberately decided they did not want to be ruled by God." From this, then, it might be concluded that the "third resurrection," after all, was not really needed. Neither is it scriptural.

CHAPTER XIII

"YOU WILL ACTUALLY BE GOD!"

" 'The theologians' and 'higher critics' have blindly accepted the heretical and false doctrine (introduced by pagan false prophets who crept in) that the Holy Spirit is a Third Person," Armstrong has said. This cannot be true, he further declares, for the reason that "this limits God to three persons." [1]

It is most important to the Armstrong gospel that God *not* be limited to Three Persons, for at the very heart of their religion is the belief that the Godhead will, in the afterlife, be composed also of Armstrong and all his *true* disciples, if they continue in his word. To put it yet another way, Armstrong teaches that he and his followers will then "actually BE GOD, even as Jesus was and is God, and His Father, a different Person, also is God!" [2]

This idea of *being God* strikes a responsive chord in many who like the thought of somehow being equated with God. These see no error at all in believing, with all their hearts, this Armstrong promise to them: "You are setting out on a training to become CREATOR—to *become* GOD!" [3]

This part of his philosophy is expounded by Armstrong as follows:

"The PURPOSE of life is that in us God is really re-creating *His own kind—reproducing Himself* after *His* own kind—for we are, upon real conversion, actually *begotten* as sons (yet unborn) of God; then through study of God's revelation in His Word, living by His every Word, constant prayer, daily experience with trials and testings, we grow spiritually more and more like God, until, at the time of the resurrection we shall be instantaneously CHANGED from mortal into *immortal*—we shall then be BORN of God—WE SHALL THEN BE GOD!

"For the word 'God' comes to us from the Hebrew word 'Elohim,' which means the Ever-living, Eternal Creating, All-powerful, Governing KINGDOM. 'Elohim' means *one God*—not many gods. But that ONE GOD *is a* KINGDOM. There is but one true CHURCH—*one* Church, but many members! (1 Cor. 12:20).

"So it is with God.

"As an illustration, there is the mineral kingdom, the plant kingdom, the animal kingdom; and we might segregate it and designate the *human* kingdom, in this material world. Spiritually, there is the angel kingdom, and, high above all, the KINGDOM OF GOD. A human—flesh and blood—cannot enter into the Kingdom of God (John 3:6), but one BORN of God can!

"Do you really grasp it? The PURPOSE of your being alive is that finally you be BORN into the Kingdom of God, when you will actually BE GOD, even as Jesus was and is God, and His Father, a different Person, also is God!

"...When you fully grasp this tremendous, wonderful TRUTH, your mind will be filled with transcendent JOY and GLORY! It gives a NEW MEANING to life so wonderful you'll never comprehend the full heights of its splendor!" [4]

This is just another example of the need to be *theologically technical* when teaching Bible doctrine. First of all, it should be noted here, "Elohim" does not mean—as Armstrong says it does—a "Governing KINGDOM." "Elohim" means "God." It is the first of many names of the Deity. First mentioned in the very first verse of the Bible, it is used about 2,500 times in the Old Testament. It "is a plural noun in form but is singular in meaning when it refers to the true God," explains C.I. Scofield. "...The plural form of the word suggests the Trinity." [5] "The original word

Elohim, God, is certainly the plural form of *El,* or *Eloah,"* adds Bible scholar Adam Clarke, "and has long been supposed, by the most eminiently learned and pious men, to imply a plurality of Persons in the divine nature. As this plurality appears in so many parts of the sacred writings to be confined to three Persons, hence the doctrine of the Trinity, which has formed a part of the creed of all those who have been deemed sound in the faith, from the earliest ages of Christianity." [6]

If the reader will bear with a little foolishness, it can be demonstrated that "Elohim" is *not,* and could not be, a synonym for "Kingdom." The phrase "kingdom of God" occurs in numerous places throughout the New Testament, but if Armstrong's definition is to be followed, it would, grammatically speaking, have to be classified as a redundancy. It would be the same as saying "kingdom of Kingdom," or "god of God," or "elohim of Elohim," all of which are plainly superfluous.

As we have just seen, Armstrong teaches that in the future life there will be an "angel kingdom," and high above this, in fact, *high above all,* will be the Godhead, which will be composed not only of God the Father and Christ His Son, but also all redeemed Christians.

This somewhat grandiose idea is certainly not from the Bible. Such a teaching is entirely contrary to the Scriptures. It is true that in this coming kingdom, Christ will be seated *high above the angels.* The author of Hebrews was most specific on this point. He wrote: "When he (Christ) had made purification for sins, he sat down at the right hand of the Majesty on high, having become as MUCH SUPERIOR TO ANGELS as the name he has obtained is more excellent than theirs" (Hebrews 1:3-4 RSV).

This, then, is Christ's exalted place in the kingdom. What—according to the Bible—will be ours? Will we, as Armstrong maintains, also be superior to the angels and have a place above them? No. Christ Himself explained our place in His reply to the Sadducees as they questioned Him sharply on the subject of marriage in the kingdom age. He said: "The sons of this age marry and are given in marriage; but those who are accounted worthy to attain to that age and to the resurrection from the dead neither marry nor are given in marriage, for they cannot die any more, because they are EQUAL TO ANGELS and are sons of God. . ." (Luke 20:34-36 RSV).

To sum up briefly:

—Christ, taking a seat "at the right hand of the Majesty on high," is described as being MUCH SUPERIOR TO ANGELS.

—Christians, on the other hand, when they enter the kingdom, are described as being EQUAL TO ANGELS, being sons of God.

—Christians therefore will NOT be HIGH ABOVE the angels, but their EQUAL, and above all in the government WILL BE GOD.

CHAPTER XIV

A WONDERFUL TRUTH?

God created man and Himself planned man's downfall, according to the gospel preached by Armstrong. Moreover, Satan, though admittedly evil, is only following God's will, doing "exactly as God Himself originally planned!" he says. [1] If this premise is not accepted, he adds, then the only other alternative is that Satan is "himself mightier and more cunning than God." [2]

This particular doctrinal eccentricity seems to be original with Armstrong. The error is outlined in the following statement by him to his many disciples. Although several paragraphs in length, it deserves close study, for this belief is fundamental to their religion and their teaching.

"WHY," he asks, "has God allowed mankind to turn his near God-like mind and powers into perversion and destruction? WHY has God allowed mankind to bring on himself all this sorrow, unhappiness and suffering?

"Many attribute all this rebellion—this SIN—to what they call the 'original fall of man.'

"Let's dare frankly to examine the common teaching about that 'Fall.'

"The common teaching, as believed and taught by most denominations, is that God created man *perfect* and *complete,* in the very image of God—and placed him in the beautiful Garden of Eden. It is believed that GOD'S CREATION WAS FINISHED, COMPLETED! Everything was perfect.

"And God was able to do this, and to start our first parents out all right, when lo and behold! Satan succeeded in invading that peaceful and blessed retreat. He successfully *overthrew* the man. Satan succeeded in thwarting God's will—upsetting God's Plan for a happy and peaceful life for his perfected humans—alienating the man and woman from God—introducing the dreadful consequences of SIN—marring, wrecking, God's creative handiwork!

"And now, according to this popular view, God's plan for a happy life and beautiful environment for His created humans was all disarranged! Now God had to commence all over again, and formulate a *new* Plan—a PLAN *to repair the damage!*

"Redemption, then, is pictured as God's PLAN for *repairing the damage* caused by Satan in that 'original Fall' of man!

"And ever since, God has entered into a furious CONTEST with Satan. For six thousand years, God has desperately been trying to *redeem* humanity—to save, and RESTORE mankind back to a condition as good as God had originally created him, before the 'Fall.'

"That's the popular idea being widely preached today!

"WHAT'S WRONG with that picture? When stated so plainly, we can see quite clearly something is wrong!

"What are we going to do with the 'fall of man?' If this popular teaching is correct, it makes Satan more powerful than God. It makes Satan able to wreck God's perfected creation, to thwart God's will.

"And, after God in desperation has devised a Plan of Redemption, and spent some six thousand years trying to restore the original Edenic perfection, where does this picture leave us today? Why, with Satan winning the contest by a pitifully lopsided score!

". . .Can't we see that at every turn this belief *presents Satan as more powerful than God?* WHAT, then, IS THE REAL TRUTH?

"Now if Satan did *not* succeed in thwarting God's will, wrecking God's perfected and completed Creation, then the only alternative is to say that it all happened *according* to

God's will—*exactly as God Himself originally planned!*

"But do we DARE make God Himself responsible?

"We have but two alternatives! Either Satan got in there *against* God's will, and in so doing proved himself mightier and more cunning than God—or else God Himself planned and permitted it all!

"LET'S UNDERSTAND THIS!"*

He continues:

". . .Now we come to the WONDERFUL TRUTH!

"The first chapter of Genesis does not record a COMPLETED creation at all!

"Adam's creation was not finished!

"Read that amazing statement again! Be sure you *understand* it!

"CREATION is *still going on!*

"SALVATION is *not* a 'repairing of the damage'—a frustrated effort of God to restore man back to a condition *as good as* Adam, before the 'Fall'!

"Satan *did not* break into the Garden of Eden in spite of God—did not do one single thing contrary to God's great PURPOSE! All that has happened had been planned before of God—and all is progressing *exactly* as GOD WILLS.

"Oh, what a WONDERFUL TRUTH!" [3]

It should be pointed out here that Armstrong is taking issue not with the orthodox church on the matter of man's fall and expulsion from the Garden of Eden but with the account given in Genesis. It needs to be noted also that in this "picture" which he himself has painted he has grossly over-exaggerated and has added to what the Scriptures actually say on this. Furthermore, if, as he contends, Satan is doing God's will, then Armstrong must acknowledge that Satan is also keeping His commandments. Indeed, if we follow Armstrong's logic, everyone may be reckoned as an obedient son—if everything is as God originally planned it.

This "WONDERFUL TRUTH" which he believes in and teaches is based on *his* idea that when God created Adam he "was not complete." Adam lacked, he says, "the indwelling of GOD'S HOLY SPIRIT." However, God supposedly had made provision for this. Armstrong explains: "In the Garden of Eden was one 'tree' which would have supplied it! And this, God freely offered the man. But Adam and Eve had to make a CHOICE between this 'tree' which would have given them LIFE—GOD'S SPIRIT—the one thing that would fill that void, that longing of the soul—and the 'tree' which symbolized the ways of SIN. Adam made the wrong choice as, of course, God knew he would!" [4]

This is the role, according to Armstrong's version, that God played in Adam's downfall. And Armstrong himself raises this most pertinent question: "Do we DARE make God Himself responsible?" He does. He says God planned it. It was, he states in so many words, God's will that the man Adam should choose the wrong way and SIN.

"All scripture is given by inspiration of God, and is profitable for doctrine, for reproof, for correction, for instruction in righteousness," writes the Apostle Paul (II Timothy 3:16). What, then, do the Scriptures have to say about this particular Armstrong doctrine? "Let no man say when he is tempted, I am tempted of God; for GOD CANNOT BE TEMPTED with evil, NEITHER TEMPTETH HE ANY MAN," says the Epistle of James (James 1:13). This doctrine can be further disproved by Christ's own words: "How think ye?" He asked His disciples. "If a man have an hundred sheep, and one of them be gone astray, doth he not leave the ninety and nine, and goeth into the mountains, and seeketh that which is gone astray? And if so be that he find it, verily I say unto you, he rejoiceth more over that sheep than over the ninety and nine which went not astray. Even so it is not the will of your Father. . .that one of these little ones should perish." (Matthew 18:12-14)

CHAPTER XV

THE ARMSTRONG DOCTRINE ON RICHES

A little riches never hurt anyone, Armstrong tells his disciples.

"The right USE of material wealth—and of the qualities which help produce it—is NOT *wrong*. Remember, *God is no pauper!*" the proselyte is taught.

"On the contrary, the right use of wealth is fulfilling part of the very PURPOSE for which we were placed on this earth. It is helping us to *grow* in right *mental direction* and *character* to become like God—like Christ, WORTHY of being *born of the Spirit* into the Supreme, Divine, world-ruling kingdom and family of God!

"Jesus Christ said: 'Be ye therefore PERFECT, even as your Father which is in heaven is perfect' (Mat. 5:48)." [1]

To show that their teaching on this is based on the Scriptures, Armstrong's ministers often point to the patriarchs whom God chose for the founding of the Hebrew nation. These progenitors, Abraham, Isaac, Jacob, and Joseph, were men of great possessions, they declare, proving that it is within God's will for Christians to seek wealth. In fact, having wealth and using it right "is fulfilling part of the very purpose" for which the Christian is placed on this earth. This "right" use of wealth, they reason, will help us grow in the "right mental direction. . .to become like God." In addition to using the patriarchs as an example, this religious sect likes to quote two statements by Jesus in which He is said to have condoned material riches for His people.* Their favorite in this regard is John 10:10: "I am come that they might have life, and that they might have it more abundantly." The other, found in Matthew 6:33, says, "Seek ye first the kingdom of God, and his righteousness; and all these things shall be added unto you."

Many who profess to be orthodox Christians will perhaps, in this one instance, agree with Armstrong. Material wealth, so long as it is used aright, some believe, is to be desired. Others believe, however, that Christians should not be concerned with material things, other than food, clothing, and shelter. These cite Christ's statement that "a rich man shall hardly enter the kingdom of heaven," and Paul's instructions to Timothy that "if we have food and clothing, with these we shall be content" (Matthew 19:23, I Timothy 6:8 RSV). From the earliest times this matter of riches and the Christian has been debated. Which side is right? What should be the Christian's attitude toward seeking material wealth?

This is a question that each Christian must ultimately answer for himself. However, in deciding, it would be a mistake to accept the examples which Armstrong's followers use in their teaching. While it is true that the patriarchs had sizable possessions, it should be kept in mind also that God was building out of them a nation, a people for His Name. Now regarding Jesus' statement, "I am come that they might have life, and that they might have it more abundantly," the *abundance* of which He speaks here has been misinterpreted. He does not mean that He came so that we might have more material possessions. This should be obvious. And Matthew 6:33 has also been taken out of context. In the preceding verses, Jesus mentions that His disciples should take no thought of what they shall wear, eat, or drink. "But," He advises them, "seek ye first the kingdom of God, and his righteousness; and all these things shall be added unto you." This promise of the Lord extends only to providing us with food and clothing, or the necessities of life, not with material riches.

We may profit from the advice Paul gave Timothy

concerning wealth. "But they that will be rich," he wrote, "fall into temptation and a snare, and into many foolish and hurtful lusts, which drown men in destruction and perdition. For the love of money is the root of all evil: which while some coveted after, they have erred from the faith, and pierced themselves through with many sorrows. But thou, O man of God, flee these things (I Timothy 6:9-11).

It is interesting to note the difference between what Paul preached on this subject and the teaching of the Armstrong gospel.

The Apostle said, ". . .The *love* of money is the root of all evil."

Roderick C. Meredith, an Armstrong associate, writes: "The *excessive* love of money is often the cause of nearly every conceivable evil."[2]

From only a quick glance these two statements seem similar. However, a moment or two of study by the reader will reveal a vast difference in meaning.

CHAPTER XVI

MEDICINE LABELED IDOLATRY

The power of divine healing has many times been affirmed in the records of the Old Testament. In the New Testament also there are numerous accounts telling of the healing of afflictions by Jesus and His disciples. Nor was this healing by God limited to those times. Though not mentioned nearly often enough by the modern church, that power continues today, as many believing Christians can testify. Since this is so, what need has the Christian for a physician? And what should be his belief about medicine?

Some religious sects say physicians and medicine are contrary to God's will.

Such is the belief of Herbert W. Armstrong, who teaches this in his gospel.

In one of his booklets, *Does God Heal Today?* he writes: "You know, my friends, a doctor can't heal. . .And none of his drugs, or medicines, or knives can heal. There is no healing in any of them. There is only one kind of healing, and that is healing directly by the almighty God! *There is no other healing!*

"Nothing else is healing in the strictest sense. God says, 'I am the Eternal that heals you,' and He isn't going to let anyone else *heal* you. . .

"The Gentile nations had many gods. They had their *gods of medicine* as well as their gods of war. They had medicine men or doctors. Their method was to go to these human doctors who would use their medicines and their drugs and then they would pray to the god of medicine, and, they believed, the god of medicine would cause these medicines to heal.

"Now there, my friends, is where medical 'Science' (falsely so called) came from. From the heathens. . .

"Now people today misunderstand this truth entirely. So many seem to believe we should go to the doctors, then pray for God to cause their medicines to heal. They assume God raised up medical science and blessed it and works thru it. But this is merely the same old Pagan practice of idolatry though very few realize it today. Truly all nations have been DECEIVED into practicing Pagan idolatry believing it is true Christianity. . .Actually, there isn't a cure in a car-load—or a trainload—of medicine!"[1]

Armstrong teaches that God's disapproval of both physicians and medicine, as paganism, is plainly revealed in several places in the Scriptures. In this regard, he quotes to his students II Chronicles 16:12-13: "And Asa in the thirty and ninth year of his reign was diseased in his feet, until his disease was exceeding great: yet in his disease he sought not to the Lord, but to the physicians. And Asa slept with his fathers, and died in the one and fortieth year of his reign." As another illustration, he points to the account of Ahaziah's fall through the lattice of his upper chamber, and his being told by Elijah the prophet that he would die because he sent messengers to inquire of "Baal-zebub the god of Ekron" instead of praying to the God of Israel for healing (II Kings 1:2-8). And for yet another proof, he offers the example of King Hezekiah, who was healed because he *did* call upon the Lord and had faith. Of this account in II Kings 20, Armstrong quotes the first six verses:

> 1 — Now Hezekiah fell ill, and was at the point of death; the prophet Isaiah, the son of Amoz, went and gave him this message from the Eternal, "Put your affairs in order, for you are to die, not to recover." 2 — Then Hezekiah turned his face to the wall and prayed to the Eternal, 3 — "O Eternal, pray remember how loyal and whole-hearted my life has been in thy presence, and how I have done right in thy

sight!" Hezekiah wept aloud. 4 — Before Isaiah had left the courtyard, this word of the Eternal came to him, 5 — "Go back and tell Hezekiah, the prince of my people, that the Eternal, the God of his father David, declares, 'I have heard your prayers, I have seen your tears, and now I heal you; the day after to-morrow you will be able to go up to the temple of the Eternal. 6 — I will add fifteen years to your life; I will rescue both you and this city from the king of Assyria, I will defend this city for my own sake and for the sake of my servant David.' " (Moffatt)

The lesson for us in these accounts about Asa, Ahaziah, and Hezekiah is certainly clear enough. God expects His people to call upon Him in times of illness for healing. But does this mean that God is also opposed to medicine and physicians, as Armstrong claims? What does the Bible really have to say about this?

Before going to the Scriptures, it would perhaps be in order here to correct the false impression that the practice of medicine in biblical times was both unlearned and confined entirely to what Armstrong describes as "medicine men" praying to a pagan god to heal their patients. This was, of course, true in many instances, especially in the backward areas. But the legitimate practice of medicine during these times was far advanced in Egypt, which has been described as "the earliest home of medical knowledge and skill." Concerning this, F.N. Peloubet has written: "Compared with the wild countries around them, the Egyptians must have seemed incalculably advanced. The process of embalming in its fullest form must have required a knowledge of anatomy and of chemistry. Representations of early Egyptian surgery apparently occur on some of the monuments of Beni-Hassan. The teeth of the mummies when opened show a dentistry which would bear comparison with a great part of what is done today. Herodotus says that every part of the body was studied by a distinct practitioner. The reputation of Egypt's practitioners in historical times was such that both Cyrus and Darius sent to that country for physicians or surgeons." [2]

From this is would appear that in some areas at least, the medical profession was both proficient and highly regarded. We know from the Bible that Joseph was one who held doctors in high esteem, for, upon the death of the patriarch Jacob, it is recorded in Genesis 50:2, he "commanded his servants the PHYSICIANS to embalm his father." This is something he would hardly have done if these early Hebrews had held physicians in ill repute. Neither did the name *physician* have a bad connotation in Jesus' own day. The Savior even applied this name to Himself when He said, ". . .They that are whole need not a physician, but they that are sick" (Luke 5:31). Luke, author of the third Gospel, was a member of the medical profession, and Paul, in his letter to the Colossians, referred to this early Christian as "THE BELOVED PHYSICIAN" (Colossians 4:14).

As for medicine, we have some mention of it. The prophet Ezekiel, in a vision he had of the age yet to come, tells of seeing a river, upon whose banks were many trees, "and the fruit thereof shall be for meat, and the leaf thereof FOR MEDICINE" (Ezekiel 47:12). In his Proverbs, King Solomon also wrote: "A merry heart doeth good LIKE A MEDICINE: but a broken spirit drieth the bones" (Proverbs 17:22). Nor did medicine seem to be regarded as an unmentionable subject among the Jews in Jeremiah's time. It was by this prophet that this famous line was spoken: "Is there no balm in Gilead; is there no physician there?" (Jeremiah 8:22. The *balm of Gilead* is described as a resinous substance from the Meccabalsam tree which was famous for its healing qualities. And Christ Himself told of the Good Samaritan who bound up the wounds of the man whom the thieves had beaten and left half dead. In binding up the wounds, it is taken for granted that medicine was used and Jesus gives us no indication here that He disapproved.

Finally, on this subject, we return to one of Armstrong's own scriptural examples. Nowhere in the Bible is it more explicitly recorded that God approves of the use of medicine for healing than in the account of Hezekiah's illness. Armstrong quotes the first six verses. The seventh, meanwhile, has been passed over. The reader will recall that before Isaiah left the courtyard, God told him to go back and tell Hezekiah that He had heard his prayer, and would not only heal him but would also add fifteen years to his life. The prophet immediately delivered this message to the sick king. Then the account continues:

> 7 — Isaiah ordered a poultice of figs to be applied to the eruption, that he might recover. (Moffatt)

The poultice of figs, of course, was a medicine which Isaiah had Hezekiah's attendants place upon the boil.

CHAPTER XVII

NO LIFE BEYOND THE GRAVE?

Most Christians believe in a life beyond the grave. The translations of Enoch and Elijah are evidence of such a life. So is Jesus' account of Lazarus and the "rich man" in Luke chapter sixteen. Further evidence is the "Transfiguration on the Mount," in which Moses and Elijah appeared and talked with Jesus in the presence of Peter, James, and John. Besides these, there are many other Scriptures in both Testaments that support this doctrine.

We also have instances from the writings of the early church which establish beyond a doubt that Christians from the first years of Christianity believed in a life beyond physical death. This teaching was clearly stated by Clement in his *Epistle to the Corinthians,* written toward the end of the first century, in which he declares that Peter, having borne his testimony and suffering martyrdom, "went to his appointed place of glory," and that Paul also "departed from the world and went unto the holy place." [1] Ignatius looked upon the approaching hour of his death as, in reality, a passage to life. "The pangs of a *new birth* are upon me," he wrote the Christians at Rome, whither guards were bringing him for execution. Again, he told them, "It is good to set from the world unto God, *that I may rise* unto Him." [2] A similar view was held by those who witnessed the martyrdom of Polycarp. The day of his death at the stake was described by them as "his birthday." [3] Irenaeus reported that the Elders, who were disciples of the apostles, taught in his day that those who were translated were transferred to Paradise, a place which had been prepared by

God "for righteous and inspired men, whither also the Apostle Paul was carried and *heard words unspeakable,* to us at least in this present life, and that they who are translated remain there until the end of all things, preluding immortality." [4] This disciple of Polycarp also repeatedly refers to Christ's descent into the spirit world after His death on the cross to make known to the dead of former ages His redemptive work.

The Liturgy of St. James, which was used by the early church, sets forth this belief in the following words: "Remember, O Lord God, the spirits of whom we have made mention, who are of the true faith, from righteous Abel unto this day; do Thou Thyself give them rest there *in the land of the living,* in Thy kingdom, in the delight of Paradise, in the Bosom of Abraham and of Isaac and of Jacob, our holy fathers; whence pain and grief and lamentations have fled away: there the light of Thy countenance looks upon them, and gives them light for evermore." [5]

These are but a few samples of the belief that prevailed in the very earliest years of the church. There are many others. We also have this faith in immortality expressed in numerous epitaphs for the Christian dead who were buried in the catacombs of Rome. "The overwhelming testimony of the oldest Christian epitaphs," writes Philip Schaff of the catacombs inscriptions, "is that the pious dead are already in the enjoyment of peace, and this accords with the Saviour's promise to the penitent thief, and with St. Paul's desire *to depart and be with Christ, which is far better.*" [6]

Just a few of these graveyard inscriptions will illustrate the expectation of these early Christians for life after our earthly existence:

—"Alexander is not dead, but *lives* above the stars, and his body rests in this tomb."

—"Anatolius made this for his well-deserving son, who lived 7 years, 7 months and 20 days. May thy spirit rest well in God. *Pray for thy sister.*"

—"In Christ. Æstonia, a virgin; a foreigner, who lived 41 years and 8 days. She *departed from the body* on the 26th of February." [7]

There can be no doubt, then, that the early Christians believed that the individual did not cease living in the spirit after the physical death of the body.

To Armstrong, however, this is all pagan nonsense. When you die, according to his gospel, you are dead—period. Of the individual, he says, nothing remains except the dust from which he was made, and there will be no life for him until the resurrection of the dead. "Death," writes his son, Garner Ted, "is DEATH—the complete absence of life and consciousness." He adds, "Nowhere does your Bible say man HAS an immortal soul, or that there *is* a 'soul' *in* man. Rather, the Bible shows man IS a soul. That is, each soul *(nephesh,* in the Hebrew) is a *person,* and *can die.* Armstrong, however, agrees "there IS a 'spirit' in man (Job 32:8). But that spirit IS NOT THE MAN—and is not CONSCIOUS *APART* from the man." [8] Therefore, he concludes, when you die you die, and any belief contrary to this is heathen.

All this, of course, is inconsistent with the Scriptures which very plainly teach a "middle state." The translations of Enoch and Elijah point to this. The account of Lazarus and the "rich man" is Christ's own vivid description of it. When these two men died, He told His disciples, each went to a different place—the rich man to Hades and Lazarus to "Abraham's bosom." Jesus also made another most positive reference to this spirit world when He said to the repentant thief crucified with Him, "Truly, I say to you, TODAY you will be WITH ME in Paradise" (Luke 23:43 RSV).

This doctrine, which was taught by the ante-Nicene or early church, was referred to as the "middle state." It is not the same as the Roman Catholic idea of purgatory, which "was substituted for Paradise," and which was based primarily on the Scripture passage in I Corinthians 3:13, 15, in which the term *ignis purgatoruis* appears, "the fire shall try every man's work of what sort it is. . .but he himself shall be saved; *yet so as by fire.*" Moreover, the purgatory doctrine, which also incorporates both the teaching of Lazarus and the "rich man" and the Jewish tradition of Sheol, is a rather late one, not having been accepted into the Roman church until 590 A.D. Although they have some similarities, declares Schaff, "there is. . .a considerable difference. The ante-Nicene idea of the middle state of the pious excludes, or at all events ignores, the idea of penal suffering, which is an essential part of the Catholic conception of purgatory. It represents the condition of the pious as one of comparative happiness, inferior only to the perfect happiness after the resurrection."[9]

In addition to those already cited, there are several other Scriptures which specifically support this particular doctrine. Three which should prove profitable for study are given here:

> "Verily, verily, I say unto you, The hour is coming, and now is, WHEN THE DEAD shall hear the voice of the Son of God: and they that hear shall live" (John 5:25).

> For Christ also hath once suffered for sins, the just for the unjust, that he might bring us to God, being put to *death in the flesh,* but made *alive by the Spirit,* by whom also HE WENT AND PREACHED UNTO THE SPIRITS IN PRISON, who at one time were disobedient, when once the long-suffering of God waited in the days of Noah, while the ark was preparing. . .(I Peter 3:18-20 Scofield Bible).

> For, for this cause was the gospel PREACHED ALSO TO THEM THAT ARE DEAD, that they might be judged according to men in the flesh, but live according to God in the spirit (I Peter 4:6 Scofield Bible).

It goes without saying that if there is no life of the spirit apart from bodily death, then Jesus after His crucifixion went and preached to no one. If this be the case, then Peter and Luke, the authors of these passages quoted here, have, whether wilfully or otherwise, falsified the Scriptures, leading us into error. Their report, however, can be accepted with complete confidence, being found to be most consistent with Christ's own teaching on this subject.

For the reader's further edification on this subject, the following Scriptures are offered:

> But Jesus answered them, "You are wrong, because you know neither the scriptures nor the power of God...As for the resurrection of the dead, have you not read what was said to you by God, 'I AM the God of Abraham, and the God of Isaac, and the God of Jacob'? HE IS NOT GOD OF THE DEAD, BUT OF THE LIVING." And when the crowd heard it, they were ASTONISHED at his teaching (Matthew 22:29, 31-33 RSV).

> For as the body APART FROM THE SPIRIT is dead, so faith apart from works is dead (James 2:26 RSV).

In II Samuel 12:23, David speaks thus of his first son by Bathsheba, the son who had just died: "I SHALL GO TO HIM, but he will not return to me."

> The years of our life are threescore and ten,
>> or even by reason of strength fourscore;
> yet their span is but toil and trouble;
>> they are soon gone, AND WE FLY AWAY
> (Psalm 90:10 RSV).

> And all were weeping and bewailing her; but he said, "Do not weep; for she is NOT DEAD but SLEEPING." And they laughed at him, KNOWING THAT SHE WAS DEAD. But taking her by the hand he called, saying, "Child, arise." And her SPIRIT RETURNED, and she got up at once...(Luke 8:52-55 RSV).

> But that the dead ARE raised, even Moses showed, in the passage about the bush, where he calls the Lord the God of Abraham and the God of Isaac and the God of Jacob. Now HE IS NOT GOD OF THE DEAD BUT OF THE LIVING; for ALL LIVE to him (Luke 20:37-38 RSV).

> "Truly, truly, I say to you, if any one keeps my word, he WILL NEVER SEE DEATH." The Jews said to him, "Now we know that you have a demon. Abraham DIED, as did the prophets; and you say, 'If

any one keeps my word, he WILL NEVER TASTE DEATH.' Are you greater than our father Abraham, WHO DIED? And the PROPHETS DIED! Who do you claim to be?" Jesus answered, ". . .Your father Abraham rejoiced that he was to see my day; HE SAW IT and was glad" (John 8:51-54, 56 RSV).

"I am the resurrection and the life; he who believes in me, though he die, yet shall he live, and whoever lives and believes in me SHALL NEVER DIE. DO YOU BELIEVE THIS?" (John 11:25-26 RSV).

Then Jesus, crying with a loud voice, said, "Father, into thy hands I COMMIT MY SPIRIT!" (Luke 23:46 RSV).

And as they were stoning Stephen, he prayed, "Lord Jesus, RECEIVE MY SPIRIT " (Acts 7:59 RSV).

None of us lives to himself, and none of us DIES TO HIMSELF. If we live, we live to the Lord, and if we die, we die to the Lord; so then, whether WE LIVE or whether WE DIE, we are the Lord's. For to this end Christ died and lived again, that he might be Lord both of the DEAD AND OF THE LIVING (Romans 14:7-9 RSV).

So we are always of good courage; we know that while we are AT HOME IN THE BODY we are AWAY FROM THE LORD. . .And we would rather be AWAY FROM THE BODY and AT HOME WITH THE LORD. So whether we are at home or away, we make it our aim to please him (II Corinthians 5:6, 8-9 RSV).

For God has not destined us for wrath, but to obtain salvation through our Lord Jesus Christ, who died for us so that whether WE WAKE OR SLEEP, we might LIVE WITH HIM (I Thessalonians 5:9-10 RSV).

Therefore I intend always to remind you of these things, though you know them and are established in the truth that you have. I think it right, as long as I am in the body, to arouse you by way of reminder, since I know that the PUTTING OFF OF MY BODY will be soon, as our Lord Jesus showed me. And I WILL SEE TO IT that AFTER MY DEPARTURE you may be able at any time to recall these things (II Peter 1:12-15 RSV).

"Truly, truly, I say to you, he who believes HAS ETERNAL LIFE " (John 6:47 RSV).

For to me to live is Christ, and TO DIE IS GAIN (Philippians 1:21 RSV).

My desire IS TO DEPART and BE WITH CHRIST, for that is far better. But to remain in the flesh is more necessary on your account (Philippians 1:23-24 RSV).

CHAPTER XVIII

FINDING THE TRUE CHURCH

Armstrong's errors have not all been discussed in the preceding chapters. The author's files contain detailed studies of many other false teachings of this sect. However, our limited space will not permit a review of these. They would lend additional weight to the evidence already presented against the false gospel taught by Armstrong.

As should be obvious to the reader, most of these beliefs of Armstrong are quite contrary to what the Bible actually teaches, and they are in direct opposition to the fundamental teachings of orthodox Christianity. Thus, one who becomes an Armstrong disciple, or even a casual follower of this movement, takes a very serious step. Because this is so, those who embrace these religious tenets would be well advised to make a very careful study and appraisal of this one man's beliefs.

In this book, we have been concerned mainly with those doctrines of the sect which plainly show the foundation upon which their religion is built. Some of these beliefs, while in error, would not be deemed serious errors. For instance, whether you choose to believe that life exists or does not exist beyond the grave until the great resurrection, whether you shun or accept medical or surgical treatment for diseases, whether you prefer to partake of the Lord's Supper only at the annual Passover, as the Armstrong church does, or more frequently as most orthodox churches do, whether you hold that the cruxifixion of Christ was on a Wednesday or a Friday, or whether you celebrate His resurrection on the seventh day of the week or on the first—all these are doctrines which do not affect your salvation, in the author's opinion. Minor differences in beliefs have always existed between Christians, as a reading of the New Testament Scriptures plainly reveals, but these, as long as they do not subtract anything from the glory of God and His righteousness by which we are saved, will not disqualify the Christian from his place in the coming Kingdom.

In addition to those mentioned above, however, there are some doctrines taught by Armstrong that are not at all compatible with orthodox Christianity. It might be to the advantage of the reader to briefly review a few of these which are found to be most serious.

It is the author's opinion, reached after many months of research into the history of the Early Church, that the Christian, in the freedom he now has, can observe or not observe the Sabbath, as he chooses, so long as he does not base this observance on the legalistic demands of the Fourth Commandment. Those who do want to place themselves under the Fourth Commandment are in very real danger of returning to the bondage of the Law given at MOUNT SINAI, the Law from which God, according to His love and His grace, has delivered us. It was on this very point that the Apostle Paul expressed deep concern to the churches of Galatia, which was then being troubled by the Judaizers. He wrote: "But now, after that ye have known God, or rather are known of God, how turn ye again to the weak and beggarly elements, whereunto ye desire again to be in bondage? Ye observe days, and months, and times, and years. I am afraid of you, lest I have bestowed upon you labour in vain" (Galatians 4:9-11).

This warning by Paul is just as timely today for those being taught that the Sabbath *must* be observed as it was for the Galatians who were being similarly instructed.

The Armstrong teaching on the Law is in very grave error. Members of this sect, as we have seen, like to think of themselves as "within the Law," rather than "under the Law." What terminology they prefer to use to describe their relationship to the Mosaic Law given at MOUNT SINAI is not important. The fact that they have willingly placed themselves and their following under its bondage speaks for itself. As we have seen, their doctrines on *justification* and *grace* hold that one can receive forgiveness for his past sins only at the moment of his conversion. This forgiveness, they say, is God's grace.[1] In their teaching, there is no forgiveness after this moment at conversion, but then, according to their beliefs, none is needed since they are able to "live, from here on, righteously, happily." [2]

The Lord, they have stated, imputes His righteousness to no one. [3] In this, they have once more disregarded the Scriptures, for Paul, in his letter to the Romans, wrote: "Even as David also describeth the blessedness of the man, unto whom God IMPUTETH RIGHTEOUSNESS without works, saying, Blessed are they whose iniquities are forgiven, and whose sins are covered" (Romans 4:6-7).

The Bible teaches in numerous places that it is by His righteousness that we are saved, not by our own, lest we have reason to boast. The author suggests it is vanity and pride in a man that deceives him into believing that he is able, in any way, to assure his salvation by his own works and his own righteousness. Of salvation, the Bible declares: "It is the gift of God" (Ephesians 2:8).

Any follower of Armstrong's teachings should examine very closely his belief that there is no Trinity—that the Godhead is composed of only the Father and the Son. This is heresy.

The most abominable of all the teachings of this sect, however, is their claim that Satan is doing the Lord's will "exactly as God Himself originally planned!"[4] No true convert to the Christian faith will entertain such a thought, much less hold it as a belief. Indeed, this one statement should provide ample proof of the true nature of this sect, and anyone truly seeking the kingdom of God should accept it as a clear warning and flee.

Based upon my own experience with this sect and my acquaintance with other converts, I can truthfully say that the overwhelming majority of Armstrong's followers are, first of all, people who have a zeal for God; they are also people who are disillusioned with the modern physical church and its hypocrisy; consequently, they seek for the *true* church. The dedication of the Armstrong people to the practice of their religion, the high moral standards they hold to, and their wholesomeness, along with their very interesting Bible study courses, cannot but help attract many sincere *would-be* Christians into their cult. As a result, some of the finest people are being taken from the established *physical* church, where, in these last days, they are sorely needed.

I hold no bitterness or resentment toward the Armstrong people. My personal feeling toward them is one of sorrow, for they have deceived themselves into believing they serve God. But like the dedicated Buddhist, Hindu or Muslim, they serve another. In my own case, my association with them, my study under them, then the very lengthy and exhaustive Bible study and library research that was required to free myself from their teachings has given me an understanding of the Holy Scriptures and its true doctrines which I might not have otherwise obtained and which I find priceless.

In joining the Armstrong sect, I sought for the *true* Church. When I left them, I found *it*. The *true* Church is not a physical building. It is not made by human hands putting together brick, mortar and lumber. The Church of which Christ spoke is a *spiritual* Church. In this Church there are no hypocrites, no factions, no bickerings, for we are all of one accord, called in peace to serve Him; neither is this body of Christ subject to being "tossed to and fro, and carried about with every wind of doctrine, by the sleight of men, and cunning craftiness, whereby they lie in wait to deceive" (Ephesians 4:14), for members of the *true* Church have always been led by the Holy Spirit.

It is my hope that, by His grace, God will help you find His *true* Church.

APPENDIX I

Jesus holds Last Supper with disciples just before sunset.

Jesus arrested, brought before Caiaphas and the Sanhedrin where He is questioned during the night hours.

When early morning came, the chief priests and elders delivered Jesus to Pontius Pilate, who sent Him to Herod who returned Him to Pilate's jurisdiction, where the chief priests and rulers prevailed upon the governor to crucify the Galilean. At 9 a.m., Jesus was nailed to the cross.

At 3 p.m. Jesus cried out and gave up the ghost. Between 3 and 6 p.m., Joseph of Arimathea asked Pilate for body.

Jesus buried as the HIGH DAY sabbath "was just beginning" (Luke 23:54). This was the time the women from Galilee saw the tomb and how He was laid, and then went to their homes to observe the high sabbath which had already begun. They could not have prepared spices or brought them until the day was over, it being a SABBATH.

The only other recorded activity on this high sabbath is that of the chief priests and pharisees appearing before Pilate to ask that the tomb be made secure "until the *third* day . . . " (Matt. 27:64).

The Feast Day Sabbath Ends.

This sunset marks the *first* full day Christ has been in the tomb.

Sometime during the regular trading hours of this second day of preparation, the feast day sabbath over, Mary Magdalene, and Mary, the mother of James, and Salome BOUGHT spices, which could not have been purchased until the sabbath was ended, and returned home to prepare them with ointments.

This sunset marks the *second* full day of Christ's entombment.

This sunset also ushered in the weekly Sabbath. The spices, having been purchased and prepared the previous day, Mary Magdalene and the other women *again* "rested according to the commandment" (Luke 23:56).

This sunset marks the *third* full day of Christ's entombment, after which Christ arose from the dead.

At early dawn, Mary Magdalene, Joanna, and Mary, the mother of James, "and certain others" went to the tomb, taking with them the spices which they had bought and prepared on Friday, but they found the stone rolled away, and the tomb empty (Luke 24:1-2).

Timeline (left margin)

TUESDAY		
WEDNESDAY	(Day of Preparation)	At sunset Jewish Day begins
THURSDAY	(High Day Sabbath)	At sunset Thursday begins
FRIDAY	(Day of Preparation)	At sunset Friday begins
SATURDAY	(Weekly Sabbath)	At sunset Sabbath begins
SUNDAY	(1st Day of Week)	At sunset Sabbath begins 1st Day of Week begins
		At sunset 1st Day of Week begins

- 110 -

NOTES

Page 8

* He has reference to Matthew 24:14 and Mark 13:10.

Page 21

* Jesus speaks on this same subject in Luke 14:26, and this is another verse which has caused some to stumble, not understanding. But compare Matthew 10:37 for His meaning.

Page 22

* Full capitals in this passage of Scripture and in others in this volume are my own.

Page 43

* Other sects that keep the Sabbath, such as the Seventh Day Adventists, will not receive the "mark of the beast," since they do not worship on Sunday, but neither will they inherit the kingdom, according to Armstrong's gospel. This position is set forth by one of their writers as follows: "There are *several* churches which believe in keeping the *fourth commandment.* But most of these churches—in their teaching and practice—directly BREAK one or more of the *other* commandments. Jesus founded only ONE church (Mat. 16:18), and it *alone* keeps ALL of God's commandments." (Roderick C. Meredith, *The Ten Commandments,* p. 32.)

Page 48

* Lit., "On the Lord's day of the Lord," a pleonastic expression to present the idea that the Sunday is very specially set aside to honor the Lord.

Page 49

* "Ignatius, surnamed Theophorus, stood at the head of the Church at Antioch at the close of the first century and the beginning of the second, and was thus contemporaneous with Clement of Rome and Simeon of Jerusalem," declares Philip Schaff. ". . .Tradition differs concerning the first episcopal succession of Antioch, making Ignatius either the second or the first bishop of this church after Peter, and calling him now a disciple of Peter, now of Paul, now of John. The Apostolic Constitutions intimate that Evodius and Ignatius presided contemporaneously over that church, the first being ordained by Peter, the second by Paul. Baronius and others suppose the one to have been the bishop of the Jewish, the other the Gentile converts." (Philip Schaff, *History of the Christian Church* [Grand Rapids, Mich.: Eerdmans] II, 653-54.)

** This is not the same Barnabas who traveled with Paul, most Bible scholars believe, although the letter's author was so identified by Clement of Alexander who quoted from it freely at the close of the second century. It is generally believed that the epistle was written early in the second century and that its author was a church leader who resided at Alexandria.

*** The full text on Barnabas' view of the *true* Sabbath is as follows: "Moreover concerning the sabbath likewise it is written in the Ten Words, in which He spake to Moses face to face on Mount Sinai: *And ye shall hallow the sabbath of the Lord with pure hands and with a pure heart.* And in another place He saith: *If My sons observe the sabbath, then I will bestow My mercy upon them.* Of the sabbath He speaketh in the beginning of the creation: *And God made the works of His hands in six days, and He ended on the seventh day, and rested on it, and He hallowed it.* Give heed, children, what this meaneth: *He ended in six days.* He meaneth this, that in six thousand years the Lord shall bring all things to an end; for the day with Him signifieth a thousand years; and this He himself beareth me witness, saying: *Behold, the day of the Lord shall be as a thousand years.* Therefore, children, in six days, that is in six thousand years, everything shall come to an end. *And He rested on the seventh day.* This He meaneth: when His Son shall come, and shall abolish the time of the Lawless One, and shall judge the ungodly, and shall change the sun and the moon and the stars, then shall He truly rest on the seventh day. Yea and furthermore He saith: *Thou shalt hallow it with pure hands and with a pure heart.* If therefore a man is able now to hallow the day which God·hallowed, though he be pure in heart, we have gone utterly astray. But if after all then and not till then shall we truly rest and hallow it, when we shall ourselves be able to do so after being justified and receiving the promise, when iniquity is no more and all things have been made new by the Lord, we shall be able to hallow it then, because we ourselves shall have been hallowed first. Finally He saith to them: *Your new moons and your sabbaths I cannot away with.* Ye see what is His meaning: it is not your present sabbaths that are acceptable [unto Me], but the sabbath which I have made, in the which, when I have set all things at rest, I will make the beginning of the eighth day which is the beginning of another world. Wherefore also we keep the eighth day for rejoicing, in the which also Jesus rose from the dead, and having been manifested ascended into the heavens." *(Epistle of Barnabas,* c. 15, quoted from *The Apostolic Fathers,* by J.B. Lightfoot. [Grand Rapids, Mich.: Baker Book House, 1956], pp. 151-152.)

Page 57

* See Genesis 1:5, 8, 13, etc.

Page 58

* The Jewish day had two evenings, one of which corresponds to our afternoon. Adam Clarke explains the Jewish day in this manner: "The Jews divided the day into morning and evening: till the sun passed the meridian all was morning or forenoon; after that, all was afternoon or evening. Their first evening began just after twelve o'clock, and continued till sunset; their second evening began at sunset and continued till night, i.e., during the whole time of twilight; between twelve o'clock, therefore, and the termination of twilight, the passover was to be offered." *(Adam Clarke's Commentary,* p. 108.) See Exodus 12:6.

* During the time I kept the Sabbath as an Armstrong disciple I came across the booklet, *Who Changed the Sabbath?* It was in it that I finally, after several readings, began to see the Armstrong error. I commend it to you for your study. This series of messages was delivered on the Radio Bible Class broadcast by Richard W. DeHaan, Radio Bible Class, Grand Rapids, Michigan, U.S.A.

* See Romans 8:16, 26; I Peter 1:11.

* The reader's attention is called here to the fact that there is a vast difference between permitting all this to happen and the planning it. The reader should not be limited by the two alternatives mentioned here by Armstrong. There are at least a few others which have long been discussed by Bible scholars. It is not, therefore, an either/or choice.

* See "Can a Wealthy Person Become a Christian?" by R.C. Meredith, *The Plain Truth,* October 1967.

REFERENCE NOTES

Chapter I

1. *The Plain Truth,* March 1968, p. 10.
2. *The Plain Truth,* January 1968, p. 2.
3. Herman L. Hoeh, "How Would You Recognize the Church Jesus Founded?" *The Plain Truth,* June 1968, p. 42.
4. *The Plain Truth,* August 1968, p. 1, 44.
5. *The Plain Truth,* August 1969, p. 2.
6. *The Plain Truth,* January 1959, p. 3.
7. *Loc. cit.*
8. Herbert W. Armstrong, *Easter Is Pagan!* (Pasadena, Calif.: Ambassador College), p. 9.
9. *Ibid.,* p. 7-8.
10. *The Plain Truth,* July 1967, p. 47.

Chapter II

1. Hoeh, *loc. cit.*
2. *The Plain Truth,* January 1969, p. 1, 30.
3. *Ambassador College Bible Correspondence Course,* Lesson 7 (Pasadena, Calif.: Ambassador College), p. 12.

Chapter IV

1. Garner Ted Armstrong, *What Is Real Repentance?* (Pasadena, Calif.: Ambassador College, 1959), p. 2.
2. *Loc. cit.*
3. *Loc. cit.*

Chapter V

1. *The Plain Truth,* June 1967, p. 2.

Chapter VI

1. Garner Ted Armstrong, "Are You 'Under' the Law?" *The Plain Truth,* November 1967, p. 11.
2. Samuel Sandmel, *The Genius of Paul* (New York: Farrar, Straus and Cudahy, 1958), pp. 37-142.
3. *Loc. cit.*
4. *The New Scofield Reference Bible* (New York: Oxford University Press, 1967), p. 1347.
5. M.R. DeHaan, M.D., *Dead to the Law* (Grand Rapids, Michigan: Radio Bible Class), pp. 16-22.

Chapter VII

1. Roderick C. Meredith, *The Ten Commandments* (Pasadena, Calif.: Ambassador College, 1960), p. 33.
2. *Loc. cit.*
3. *Ibid.,* p. 29.
4. H.W. Armstrong, *What Do You Mean—Salvation?* (Pasadena, Calif.: Ambassador College, 1961), p. 17.
5. Philip Schaff, *History of the Christian Church* (Grand Rapids, Michigan: Eerdmans, 1960), II, 201-202.
6. *Ibid.,* pp. 202-203.
7. H.W. Armstrong, *Which Day Is The Sabbath?* (Pasadena, Calif.: Ambassador College, 1952), p. 8.

8. *Ibid.,* p. 17.

9. Schaff, *op. cit.,* p. 201.

10. F.L. Cross, *The Early Christian Fathers* (London: Gerald Duckworth & Co., Ltd., 1960), pp. 8, 11.

11. *Ancient Christian Writers* (London: Longmans, Green and Co., Ltd., 1948), VI, 23.

12. *Epistle to the Magnesians,* c. 9.

13. *Epistle of Barnabas,* c. 15.

14. *Letter to Trajan,* Ep. X. 97.

15. James Hastings, editor, *Encyclopaedia of Religion and Ethics* (New York: Charles Scribner's Sons, 1927).

16. *Against Heresies* IV. 16.

17. Cross, *op. cit.,* p. 110.

18. *Apology to Caesar,* c. 150.

19. *Loc. cit.*

20. Eusebius, *Ecclesiastical History* (Grand Rapids, Michigan: Baker Book House, 1955), Book III, Chap. XXVII, pp. 112-113.

Chapter VIII

1. Schaff, *op. cit.,* II, 205.

2. *Loc. cit.*

3. Jack Finegan, *The Handbook of Bible Chronology* (Princeton, New Jersey: Princeton University Press, 1964), p. 288.

4. A. Gilmore, "Date and Significance of the Last Supper," *Scottish Journal of Theology,* September, 1961, pp. 256-259, 264-268.

5. *Loc. cit.*

6. *Loc. cit.*

7. Maurice Goguel, *Life of Jesus* (New York: Barnes and Noble, 1948).

Chapter IX

1. *New York Times* News Service, October 11, 1969.

2. Schaff, *op. cit.,* II, 236.

3. H.W. Armstrong, *Which Day Is the Sabbath?* p. 11.

4. *Ibid.,* p. 12.

5. Schaff, *op. cit.,* I, 474.

6. *Epistle to the Ephesians,* quoted from *Readings in Church History,* Colman J. Barry, editor (Glen Rock, New Jersey: Newman, 1960), I, 23.

7. *Apology to Caesar,* c. 150.

Chapter X

1. *The Plain Truth,* February 1960, p. 26.

2. *The Plain Truth,* February 1962, p. 45.

3. Schaff, *op. cit.,* II, 560.

4. *Ibid.,* pp. 571-80.

5. *Ibid.,* p. 561.

6. *The Martyrdom of Polycarp,* quoted from the *Ancient Christian Writers,* p. 97.

7. *Apology to Caesar,* I. 13.

8. Schaff, *op. cit.,* II, 536.

Chapter XI

1. G.T. Armstrong, "Are You 'Under' the Law?" p.11.

2. *Ibid.*, p. 10.
3. H.W. Armstrong, *What Do You Mean—Salvation?* p. 17.
4. *Ibid.*, p. 18.
5. *Ibid.*, pp. 17-18, 20-21.
6. Schaff, *op. cit.*, I, 536.
7. *Ibid.*, p. 537.

Chapter XII
1. H.W. Armstrong, *What Do You Mean—Salvation?* p. 15.
2. Herbert Lockyer, *All the Doctrines of the Bible* (Grand Rapids, Michigan: Zondervan, 1964), p. 162.
3. H.W. Armstrong, *What Do You Mean. . ."The Unpardonable Sin"?* (Pasadena, Calif.: Ambassador College, 1967), p. 6.
4. H.W. Armstrong, *Predestination—Does the Bible Teach It?* (Pasadena, Calif.: Ambassador College, 1957), p. 12.
5. C.P. Meredith, *If You Die. . .Will You Live Again?* (Pasadena, Calif.: Ambassador College, 1957), p. 3.
6. *Loc. cit.*
7. *Ibid.*, p. 4.

Chapter XIII
1. *The Plain Truth,* February 1962, p. 45.
2. H.W. Armstrong, *Why Were You Born?* (Pasadena, Calif.: Ambassador College, 1957), p. 21.
3. *Ibid.*, p. 22.
4. *Ibid.*, pp. 21-22.
5. *The New Scofield Reference Bible,* p. 1.
6. *Adam Clarke's Commentary* (Grand Rapids, Michigan: Baker Book House, 1967), p. 16.

Chapter XIV
1. H.W. Armstrong, *Why Were You Born?* p. 8.
2. *Loc. cit.*
3. *Ibid.*, pp. 7-9.
4. *Ibid.*, p. 10.

Chapter XV
1. Roderick C. Meredith, "Can A Wealthy Person Become A Christian?" *The Plain Truth,* October 1967, p. 10.
2. *Ibid.*, p. 11.

Chapter XVI
1. H.W. Armstrong, *Does God Heal Today?* (Pasadena, Calif.: Ambassador College, 1952), pp. 4-6, 11.
2. *Peloubet's Bible Dictionary* (Philadelphia: Universal Book and Bible House, 1947), p. 396.

Chapter XVII
1. *Epistle to the Corinthians,* c. 5.
2. *Epistle to the Romans,* c. 6, c. 2.
3. *The Martyrdom of St. Polycarp,* c. 18.
4. *Irenaeus* XIII, v. 5. 1.
5. Schaff, *op. cit.,* II, 604.
6. *Ibid.*, II, 303.
7. *Ibid.*, II, 301, 304.
8. Garner Ted Armstrong, "When You Die—Then What Happens?"

The Plain Truth, June 1967, pp. 18, 22.
   9. Schaff, *op. cit.,* II, 605.

Chapter XVIII
   1. Garner Ted Armstrong, "Are You 'Under' the Law?" p.11.
   2. H.W. Armstrong, *What Do You Mean—Salvation?* p. 18.
   3. *Ibid.,* p. 17-18, 20-21.
   4. H.W. Armstrong, *Why Were You Born?* p. 8.